Excellence: An American Treasury

Privately Published by Westvaco, Christmas 1988

Glow by Josef Albers USA 15c
Learning
never ends

Glow by Josef Albers USA 15c
Learning
never ends

Glow by Josef Albers USA 15c
Learning
never ends

Glow by Josef Albers USA 15c
Learning
never ends

An American Treasury

Excellence

Citius, altius, fortius
Swifter, higher, stronger
Olympic motto

Frontispiece I
Learning never ends, 1980
designed by Bradbury Thompson

Frontispiece II
Homage to the Square: Glow, 1966
by Josef Albers

Westvaco

Foreword

In the language of America, the word *excellence*, derived from the Latin *excellentia*, commands a distinguished place of honor.

There are simpler words, like good, better and best. There are fancier words, like elegant and exquisite. There are melodious words, like marvelous and magnificent. There are combinations of words, like top notch, first rate, above par, world class, or simply number one. But, like a precious gem, worth a million times more than an ordinary commodity, even gold, or, for that matter, an ordinary word, like mediocre, shoddy, late or lazy, the word *excellence* stands alone, prized, revered, idolized.

That same word *excellence* has been a very important word in the vocabulary of Westvaco people for many years. *Excellence* is a word which reflects in many ways our company's basic beliefs, a word which we do not take lightly nor use indiscriminately. For example, as we prepared to enter the present decade, in 1980 we gave very careful thought, as we always do, to precisely the right word or combinations of words to use as the theme for our annual report that year. After long consideration we knew, without question, exactly what we wanted to say. As a result of this labor of thought, *Excellence for the Eighties* appeared on the cover of our 1980 annual report, a theme which implies an awfully big responsibility, a corporate commitment to reach ambitious goals.

Today we have no regrets in having used these strong words of commitment. As we reflect on the progress the company has made during the challenging years which have passed since then, it is with considerable pride we can say that the Westvaco organization was equal to the task. *Excellence for the Eighties* proved to be more than a commitment. The commitment is becoming a reality.

Commensurate thought and consideration have been given to the use of the word *excellence* as the title for our 1988 Christmas book. As the words for our annual report at the beginning of the decade seemed exactly right then, our favorite word wears well, and so we are using it again. First of all, the word *excellence* accurately reflects a key competitive strength which our management team has worked long and hard to instill in every unit throughout Westvaco. It is simply the desire to be best, to do things better, to strive for excellence, to create something of unique and lasting value that others cannot easily match.

There is another reason why the word *excellence* seems exactly right for our book title this year. It seems to be exactly the word needed to help provide recognition and respect for the hard work and dedicated effort that went into building Westvaco's fundamental strengths over many years. The company was founded on October 19, 1888 near what is now the town of Luke, Maryland. And so, this year, we are commemorating Westvaco's centennial. In marking the occasion in the months just passed, it seemed logical again to use the word we hold in such high regard, this time as part of the company's centennial theme.

A Pledge of Excellence: Our Second 100 Years, represents a continuing dedication of Westvaco people today in serving our customers and in rewarding our shareholders. The theme also reflects the importance the company places in looking ahead and our faith in the future.

As we approached the creative task of preparing the volume, we decided that it would be interesting to bring together in one place a variety of thoughts on the subject of excellence expressed by others throughout American history. We had had some experience in compiling an anthology of this kind before. In 1984 we produced *America: An Affirmation of Faith*, a collection of patriotic expressions about the country. For this edition we decided that we would simply retrace our steps, only this time concentrating our sights on the subject of excellence. However, we found that, while researching the book on America was by nature straightforward, the commentaries on the subject of excellence were frequently hidden within subject material bearing other identity. Not every author is inclined to use the title *excellence* or even use the word *excellence* as the centerpiece of a thesis on the virtues of high achievement.

What we did discover, however, seemed to us as to be of even greater potential interest to the reader. We began to find many examples, simply good common sense advice on how to do a variety of interesting things exceedingly well. For example, Ernest Hemingway in *Monologue to the Maestro* advises an aspiring writer on what it will take to succeed. The language is rather colorful, we might add, and the scene takes place on a fishing boat. Athletes, we find, have their own special way of expressing their views on excellence. Coach Vince Lombardi's creed and Knute Rockne's talk to a group of Studebaker salesmen are classics on rewards of extra effort, teamwork and competitive spirit.

As a change of pace, we decided not to have everything in the book be a "sermonette" on excellence, and so we added an occasional poem, *Paddle Your Own Canoe* by Sarah Bolton, for example, short quotations with inspirational tones, and something else we found to be very interesting.

During our research, we discovered a number of things that to us seem to epitomize a special brand of American excellence. Samuel Clemens describes an American innovation in postal service in *The Pony Express*. Samuel Eliot Morison celebrates the wonderful American clipper ships. Red Smith in *Miracle of Coogan's Bluff* recants the greatest moment in baseball, which will undoubtedly prove to be of interest to a number of our customers and Westvaco friends who know the real Bobby Thomson. Following his famous baseball career, Bobby served as a valued member of our organization for many years.

We found something else well worth preserving in the lore of excellence. Some of the best advice on how to succeed in business, we discovered, has been presented over the years in the advertisements prepared by advertising agencies themselves to promote their own services. *Why Leaders Win Price Wars* is one example. *How to Grow a Great Salesman* and *Written After Hours* are two others. We've also included a marvelous piece by David Ogilvy who compares the work of a master chef with the sensitive task of managing a creative organization. *The Penalty of Leadership* by Cadillac and *The Priceless Ingredient* by Squibb are also among the greatest advertisements of all time.

Not surprising, President Harry Truman has no nonsense advice for students. Chuck Yeager stresses the importance of experience. *The Little Engine That Could* is included for sentimental reasons. It was the first story read to many of us long before we could read ourselves.

Ernie Pyle, Walt Disney, Helen Keller, Dale Carnegie and John Steinbeck are also among the one hundred different entries which we have assembled. Should you wonder why we selected precisely one hundred, it simply seemed an appropriate editorial pun to make in celebration of our centennial. For added measure, we have also taken the ten letters of the word *excellence* and placed each letter individually into a graphic segment on the spine. Each letter represents a decade of Westvaco progress.

Before completing the assignment, we discovered that our selections for the volume then in hand added up to precisely ninety-nine. We were one message short of the mark. We would need one more contribution of value on the subject of excellence in order to equal our centennial goal of an even one hundred. It was then that we remembered a source of wisdom for our time, a contemporary American, we had nearly forgotten. A tall, lean, rather quiet man readily came to mind, a cardiologist, a writer, an athlete, a man who holds many of the beliefs we admire.

Our attention was first drawn to this man nearly a decade ago. He stood quietly on the Verrazano Bridge. He waited for the moment for which he had trained so long and hard. It was the start line for the New York City Marathon. He told us his name was George Sheehan. George looked as if he might be in his late forties. Actually, as we learned later he was barely on the sunny side of sixty. Some of the people on the bridge that day knew him well. To many others at home watching the coverage on ABC Sports, he was, like the rest of us, unpublicized, uncelebrated, and except for a small nucleus within the running fraternity, unknown. Few of us at the time were aware of how *Sports Illustrated* had already begun to react to the man's unusual wit and wisdom. "He may be our most important philosopher of sport," an editor of the magazine had said.

On that day, however, few of us, if any, were contemplating the musings of a contemporary sports philosopher. If anything, we were concentrating on the stark reality of being on the Verrazano Bridge. It was ten o'clock on a Sunday morning. It was cold, windy and wet, and for some of us, a time for doubt. Why in the name of common sense were we there? We felt alone. Others, too, had their own private demons to confront. Yet, we were not alone. More than ten thousand others were standing on that bridge, each contemplating the meaning of excellence and a commitment to pursue it.

Two silver blimps, ghost-like, circled above, barely visible in the thick overcast. At first, the blimps seemed to have a calming effect on the men and women below. Then a brace of helicopters, armed with a video link to the outside world began to circle and dart about nervously, as if playing tag around the massive towers which guard the Staten Island end of the bridge. The choppers chattered incessantly. They seemed to take away the calm. We were like race horses being positioned at the gate.

The moment of truth faced us squarely. Sixty seconds to go. Then five...four...three...two...one...the Army howitzer signaled the start. The mass of humanity, driving forward, an awesome surge of power, awakening the bridge like a sleeping giant from a year's slumber, its undulating skin, the ribbon of concrete, suspended by cables began to shiver perceptively. Here we are, trying to run through a solid wall of humanity on what feels like an endless trampoline, and then we reach the two-mile mark and open road, but the challenge has just begun. As if we need a constant reminder of human imperfection, electronic digital recorders in clear view along the course seem to digitize even faster than they did last year. The time splits being called out by the volunteers along the course strip away for many the vision of a personal best that day.

George Sheehan had long ago learned the truth about why we were undergoing the ordeal of twenty-six miles, three hundred and eighty-five yards. "We were not created to be spectators," he said, "not made to be onlookers, nor born to be bystanders. You and I cannot view life as a theatergoer would, pleased or displeased by what unfolds. You, as well as I, are producer, playwright, actor, making, creating and living the drama on stage. Life must be lived. Acted out. The play we are in is our own."

Across the blue finish line in Central Park, the wisdom of this same man, this patriarch of the marathon, a sport which bears the distinction of stretching a human being to the absolute limit, would help answer the inevitable question on the minds of many who had conquered the course for the first time that day. What do I do next? And he would answer the question for his fellow athletes the same as he would answer the question for himself. "No matter what I have done," he would say, "there is still more to do. No matter how well it has been done, it can be done better. Everything I do must be aimed at that, aimed at being a masterpiece. The things I write, the races I run, each day I live. There can be no other way. If you take less than that view, you're finished."

What more can be said? What better way to close out our search for the last entry. What better way to introduce *Excellence: An American Treasury*.

For our readers of long duration who might by now have lost count, this is the thirty-first volume in the Westvaco Americana series of limited editions which the company first began publishing in 1958. As always, it is our way of expressing deep appreciation for the continuing loyalty of the people in all walks of life who provide encouragement and support for the company's continuing progress.

Finally, as a reader of this year's Christmas book, we hope you will find the carefully crafted words of wisdom of the one hundred American apostles of excellence as inspirational as we did in bringing them together in this unusual, if not unforgettable conclave. From what we can determine, the potpourri of philosophy which we have presented represents a unique way to deal with a subject of considerable subjectivity, one frequently defined by those who seek precision in our language as being indefinable, if not unattainable.

When all is said and done, we also hope that, in your own mind, you will always freely associate Westvaco, the company that brought you this book on excellence, with Westvaco, the company that continually strives to achieve excellence in serving its customers, rewarding its shareholders, and in meeting its responsibilities as a good corporate citizen.

If this book contributes even modestly toward that recognition, we will consider it to be a publishing success.

Contents

Excellence: An American Treasury

1   *Fortitude and Patience*

It was answered,
that all great and honorable actions
are accompanied with great difficulties
and must be enterprised and overcome
with answerable courages.
It was granted
the dangers were great,
but not desperate.
The difficulties were many,
but not invincible.
For though there were many of them likely,
yet they were not certain.
It might be sundry of the things feared
might never befall;
others by provident care
and the use of good means
might in a great measure be prevented;
and all of them
through the help of God,
by fortitude and patience,
might either be borne or overcome.
William Bradford

2   *Four Points*

Those who write
of the art of poetry teach us
that if we would write
what may be worth the reading,
we ought always,
before we begin,
to form a regular plan
and design of our piece:
otherwise,
we shall be in danger of incongruity.
I am apt to think it is the same as to life.
I have never fixed a regular design in life;
by which means
it has been a confused variety
of different scenes.
I am now entering upon a new one:
let me, therefore, make some resolutions,
and form some scheme of action,
that, henceforth,
I may live in all respects like a rational creature.

I   It is necessary
for me to be extremely frugal
for some time,
till I have paid what I owe.

II   To endeavor to speak truth
in every instance;
to give nobody expectations
that are not likely to be answered,
but aim at sincerity
in every word and action—
the most amiable excellence in a rational being.

III To apply myself industriously
     to whatever business I take in hand,
     and not divert my mind from my business
     by any foolish project of growing suddenly rich;
     for industry and patience
     are the surest means of plenty.

IV I resolve to speak ill of no man whatever,
     not even in a matter of truth;
     but rather by some means
     excuse the faults I hear charged upon others,
     and upon proper occasions
     speak all the good I know of every body.
     Benjamin Franklin, 1726

3   It is not easy
   to conceive what will be
   the greatness and importance of North America
   in a century or two...
   if the present fabric of Nature is upheld,
   and the people
   retain those bold and manly sentiments of freedom,
   which actuate them at this day.
   Philip Freneau, 1782

His mind was great and powerful,
without being of the very first order;
his penetration strong,
though not so acute as that
of a Newton, Bacon or Locke;
and as far as he saw,
no judgment was ever sounder.
It was slow in operation,
being little aided by invention or imagination,
but sure in conclusion....
Hearing all suggestions,
he selected whatever was best;
and certainly no General
ever planned his battles more judiciously.
But if deranged
during the course of the action...
he was slow in readjustment....
He was incapable of fear,
meeting personal dangers
with the calmest unconcern.

Perhaps the strongest feature
in his character was prudence,
never acting until every circumstance,
every consideration
was maturely weighed....
His integrity was most pure,
his justice the most inflexible
I have ever known,
no motives of interest or consanguinity,
of friendship or hatred,
being able to bias his decision.

He was, indeed,
in every sense of the words,
a wise, a good, and a great man.

His temper
was naturally irritable and high toned;
but reflection and resolution had obtained
a firm and habitual ascendancy over it.
If ever, however, it broke its bonds,
he was most tremendous in his wrath.

In his expenses
he was honorable, but exact;
liberal in contributions
to whatever promised utility;
but frowning and unyielding
on all visionary projects
and all unworthy calls on his charity.

His heart
was not warm in its affections;
but he exactly calculated every man's value,
and gave him a solid esteem
proportioned to it.

His person,
you know, was fine,
his stature
exactly what one would wish,
his deportment
easy, erect and noble;
the best horseman of his age,
and the most graceful figure
that could be seen on horseback.

Although in the circle of his friends,
where he might be unreserved with safety,
he took a free share in conversation,
his colloquial talents were not above mediocrity,
possessing neither copiousness of ideas,
nor fluency of words.
In public,
when called on for a sudden opinion,
he was unready, short and embarrassed.
Yet he wrote readily, rather diffusely,
in an easy and correct style.
This he had acquired
by conversation with the world,
for his education
was merely reading, writing and common arithmetic,
to which he added surveying at a later day.
His time
was employed in action chiefly,
reading little, and that
only in agriculture and English history....
His agricultural proceedings
occupied most of his leisure hours within doors.

On the whole, his character was,
in its mass, perfect,
in nothing bad,
in few points indifferent;
and it may truly be said,
that never did nature and fortune
combine more perfectly
to make a man great,
and to place him...
in an everlasting remembrance.
Thomas Jefferson of George Washington

5 The heights by great men reached and kept
  Were not attained by sudden flight,
   But they, while their companions slept,
  Were toiling upward in the night.
  Henry Wadsworth Longfellow, 1841

Go not so far out of your way
for a truer life;
keep strictly onward in that path alone
which your genius points out.
Do the things which lie nearest to you,
but which are difficult to do.

In the long run
men hit only what they aim at.
Therefore,
though they should fail immediately,
they had better aim at something high.

There is one obligation,
and that is the obligation
to obey the highest dictate.

Let me say
to you and to myself in one breath:
Cultivate the tree
which you have found to bear fruit
in your soil.
Regard not your past failures nor successes.
All the past is equally a failure and a success;
it is a success in as much as
it offers you the present opportunity.
Henry David Thoreau, c. 1841–1852

7 Voyager upon life's sea,
   To yourself be true,
   And whate'er your lot may be,
   Paddle your own canoe.
   Sarah K. Bolton, 1854

8   I Say 'Try'

I will study and prepare myself
and then someday my chance will come.

Success
does not so much depend
on external help as on self-reliance.

I don't think much of a man
who is not wiser today than he was yesterday.

Let us have faith,
let us dare to do our duty
as we understand it.

I am always for the man who wishes to work.

I say "try."

If we never try,
we shall never succeed.
Abraham Lincoln

9 Duty
   then is the sublimest word
   in our language.
   Do your duty in all things.
   You cannot do more.
   You should never wish to do less.
   Robert E. Lee

In a little while
all interest was taken up
in stretching our necks and watching
for the "pony-rider"—the fleet messenger
who sped across the continent
from St. Joe to Sacramento,
carrying letters
nineteen hundred miles in eight days!
Think of that
for perishable horse
and human flesh and blood to do!
The pony-rider
was usually a little bit of a man,
brimful of spirit and endurance.
No matter what time
of the day or night his watch came,
and no matter
whether it was winter or summer,
raining, snowing, hailing, or sleeting,
or whether his "beat" was a level straight road
or a crazy trail over mountain crags and precipices,
or whether it led through peaceful regions
or regions that swarmed with hostile Indians,
he must be always ready to leap into the saddle
and be off like the wind!
There was no idling-time for a pony-rider on duty.
He rode fifty miles without stopping,
by daylight, moonlight, starlight,
or through the blackness of darkness—
just as it happened.
He rode a splendid horse that was born for a racer
and fed and lodged like a gentleman;

kept him at his utmost speed for ten miles, and then,
as he came crashing up to the station
where stood two men
holding fast a fresh, impatient steed,
the transfer of rider and mailbag
was made in the twinkling of an eye,
and away flew the eager pair
and were out of sight
before the spectator
could get hardly the ghost of a look.
Both rider and horse went "flying light."
The rider's dress was thin, and fitted close;
he wore a "roundabout," and a skull-cap,
and tucked his pantaloons
into his boot-tops like a race-rider.
He carried no arms—
he carried nothing that was not absolutely necessary,
for even the postage on his literary freight
was worth *five dollars a letter.*
He got but little frivolous correspondence to carry—
his bag had business letters in it, mostly.
His horse was stripped of all unnecessary weight, too.
He wore a little wafer of a racing saddle,
and no visible blanket.
He wore light shoes, or none at all.
The little flat mail-pockets
strapped under the rider's thighs
would each hold about the bulk of a child's primer.
They held many
and many an important business chapter
and newspaper letter,
but these were written on paper
as airy and thin as gold-leaf, nearly,
and thus bulk and weight were economized.

The stage-coach traveled about a hundred
to a hundred and twenty-five miles a day
(twenty-four hours),
the pony-rider about two hundred and fifty.
There were about eighty pony-riders
in the saddle all the time, night and day,
stretching in a long, scattering procession
from Missouri to California,
forty flying eastward, and forty toward the west,
and among them making four hundred gallant horses
earn a stirring livelihood and see a deal of scenery
every single day in the year.

We had had a consuming desire,
from the beginning,
to see a pony-rider,
but somehow or other
all that passed us and all that met us
managed to streak by in the night,
and so we heard only a whiz and a hail,
and the swift phantom of the desert was gone
before we could get our heads out of the windows.
But now we were expecting one along every moment
and would see him in broad daylight.
Presently the driver exclaims:

"Here he comes!"

Every neck is stretched farther
and every eye strained wider.
Away across the endless dead level of the prairie
a black speck appears against the sky,
and it is plain that it moves.
Well, I should think so!

In a second or two
it becomes a horse and rider,
rising and falling, rising and falling—
sweeping toward us nearer and nearer—
growing more and more distinct,
more and more sharply defined—
nearer and still nearer,
and the flutter of the hoofs comes faintly to the ear—
another instant a whoop and a hurrah
from our upper deck,
a wave of the rider's hand,
but no reply,
and man and horse burst past our excited faces
and go swinging away
like a belated fragment of a storm!

So sudden is it all
and so like a flash of unreal fancy
that, but for the flake of white foam left quivering
and perishing on a mail sack
after the vision had flashed by and disappeared,
we might have doubted whether we had seen
any actual horse and man at all, maybe.
Samuel L. Clemens, 1872

There is a prize
which we are all aiming at,
and the more power and goodness we have,
so much more the energy of that aim.
Every human being has a right to it,
and in the pursuit
we do not stand in each other's way.
For it has a long scale of degrees,
a wide variety of views,
and every aspirant, by his success in the pursuit,
does not hinder
but helps his competitors.
I might call it completeness, but that is later,—
perhaps adjourned for ages.
I prefer to call it Greatness.
It is the fulfilment
of a natural tendency in each man.
It is a fruitful study.
It is the best tonic to the young soul.
And no man is unrelated;
therefore
we admire eminent men, not for themselves,
but as representatives.

It is very certain
that we ought not to be and shall not be contented
with any goal we have reached.
Our aim is no less than greatness;
that which invites all,
belongs to us all,—
to which we are all
sometimes untrue, cowardly, faithless,

but of which we never quite despair,
and which, in every sane moment,
we resolve to make our own.
It is also the only platform
on which all men can meet.
What anecdotes of any man
do we wish to hear or read?
Only the best.
Certainly not those in which
he was degraded to the level of dulness or vice,
but those in which
he rose above all competition
by obeying a light that shone to him alone.
This is the worthiest history of the world.
Ralph Waldo Emerson, 1883

Here is the prime condition of success,
the great secret:
concentrate your energy,
thought, and capital exclusively
upon the business in which you are engaged.
Having begun in one line,
resolve to fight it out on that line, to lead in it;
adopt every improvement,
have the best machinery,
and know the most about it.
The concerns which fail are those
which have scattered their capital, which means
that they have scattered their brains also.
They have investments in this,
or that, or the other,
here, there and everywhere.
"Don't put all your eggs in one basket" is all wrong.
I tell you "put all your eggs in one basket,
and then watch that basket."
Look round you and take notice;
men who do that do not often fail.
It is easy to watch and carry the one basket.
It is trying to carry too many baskets
that breaks most eggs in this country.
He who carries three baskets must put one on his head,
which is apt to tumble and trip him up.
One fault of the American business man
is lack of concentration.
Lastly, be not impatient, for, as Emerson says,
"no one can cheat you out of ultimate success
but yourselves."
Andrew Carnegie, 1885

No man
has earned the right to intellectual ambition
until he has learned to lay his course by a star
which he has never seen,—
to dig by the divining rod for springs
which he may never reach.

In saying this,
I point to that
which will make your study heroic.
For I say to you
in all sadness of conviction,
that to think great thoughts
you must be heroes as well as idealists.

Only when you have worked alone,—
when you have felt around you
a black gulf of solitude more isolating
than that which surrounds the dying man,
and in hope and in despair
have trusted to your own unshaken will,—
then only can you gain
the secret isolated joy of the thinker,
who knows that,
a hundred years after he is dead and forgotten,
men who have never heard of him
will be moving to the measure of his thought,—
the subtle rapture of a postponed power,
which the world knows not
because it has no external trappings,
but which to his prophetic vision
is more real than that which commands an army.

And if this joy should not be yours,
still it is only thus that you can know
that you have done what it lay in you to do,–
can say that you have lived,
and be ready for the end.
Oliver Wendell Holmes, Jr., 1886

A new episode
in American history began in 1815.
New subjects demanded new treatment,
no longer dramatic
but steadily tending to become scientific.
The traits of American character were fixed;
the rate of physical and economical growth
was established; and history, certain
that at a given distance of time
the Union would contain so many millions of people,
with wealth valued at so many millions of dollars,
became thenceforward chiefly concerned
to know what kind of people these millions were to be.
They were intelligent, but what paths
would their intelligence select?
They were quick, but what solution
of insoluble problems would quickness hurry?
They were scientific, but what control
would their science exercise over their destiny?
They were mild, but what corruptions
would their relaxations bring?
They were peaceful, but by what machinery
were their corruptions to be purged?
What interests were to vivify a society
so vast and uniform?
What ideals were to ennoble it?
What object, besides physical content,
must a democratic continent aspire to attain?

For the treatment of such questions,
history required another century of experience.
Henry Adams, c. 1889

It is not the critic who counts,
not the man
who points out how the strong man stumbled,
or where the doer of deeds
could have done them better.
The credit belongs to the man
who is actually in the arena;
whose face is marred
by dust and sweat and blood;
who strives valiantly;
who errs and comes short again and again;
who knows the great enthusiasms,
the great devotions,
and spends himself in a worthy cause;
who at the best
knows the triumph of high achievement;
and who at the worst,
if he fails,
at least fails while daring greatly;
so that his place
shall never be with those cold and timid souls
who know neither victory or defeat.
Theodore Roosevelt

16 The most important thing
    in the Olympic Games
    is not to win but to take part,
    just as the most important thing in life
    is not the triumph but the struggle.
    The essential thing
    is not to have conquered
    but to have fought well.
    The Olympic Creed, 1894

17 *The Sportsman and His Guide*

The sportsman's relation to his guide
is scarcely less close,
scarcely less sacred than that of child to mother;
for no matter how much experience
we of the city and town may have had
in the ways of the wilderness,
when we leave the beaten paths and the settlements
and head for the backwoods
with our faithful guide as sole companion,
we cannot but feel,
as we follow the unblazed trail at his side,
that compared with the trained, inborn woodcraft
of this lifelong woodsman,
we are but children in our partial knowledge
of the woods and of how to live in them....

In the fourteen seasons
which I spent here in the Adirondacks...
it has been my good fortune to bivouac
in the same camp, under the same blanket,
with scores of trusty woodsmen—
some of whom are here tonight—
on many a lonely lake,
in many a gloomy mountain pass, and under stars
that shone upon as wild, remote and beautiful regions
as sun ever set over in the Empire State;
and I can say—and it gives me pleasure to say it—
that on every occasion
I have found the hardy, keen-witted woodsmen
whom we engage in the triple capacity
of "guide, philosopher, and friend"
to be fully worthy of this wide-embracing designation....

What varied experiences
we have had together, my guide and I!
Now we are working our way, side by side,
up the rugged, forbidding slopes of Mt. Marcy—
I a stripling of fourteen,
he a stalwart weather-beaten woodsman of fifty.
Again, we are pushing our light boat
up a narrowing creek in the St. Regis
or Fish Creek waters,
or carrying it over to an isolated, little-known chain
of ponds to the southwest of Mud Lake.
Now threading the watermazes
of those wilderness ponds
between Forked Lake and Little Tupper,
or exploring the wild, trackless country
round Cold River and Mounts Seward and Santanoni.
Again, we are penetrating
the mysterious fastnesses of Indian Pass,
or descending the precipitous wall of Panther Gorge,
or wetting our feet in the immaculate waters
of Lake Tear-of-the-Clouds.
Up the broad Raquette
we sweep in our graceful guide boat—
my guide and I....
Always my guide
is the same patient, faithful, assistful companion;
bearing the burdens with me
(and bearing more than his share);
making camp at nightfall
wherever we might find ourselves;
cooking meals that kings might envy—
kindly, considerate, attentive.
Is it any wonder that the guide and the sportsman
are inseparable friends through life;

that no matter how exalted may be the social
or official rank of a sportsman,
his guide is always made to feel one with him—
on equal footing.
Scores of guides there are who have been
the campmates and have slept under one blanket
with Presidents of the United States, with statesmen,
generals, poets, philosophers, scientists—
the greatest men of the land—
nor can the greatest of the land
think it other than an honor
to share companionship with these sturdy,
resolute men of honor, courage, and tact
who of all men deserve the designation,
"Nature's noblemen."

I cannot adequately express to you in my own words
the strength of this familiar fellowship
which exists between the sportsman and his guide;
this rooted friendship
which years of separation cannot shake;
this admiration in which the man of the city
holds his brother man who has lived his life
amid the ennobling environments of the forest;
this strange, magnetic bond
which unites the city-bred woodlover and his guide.
And, so, I shall quote for you a few lines
which were written at my request, a year or two ago,
about an old guide whom most of you
have known well, by one whose name
is familiar to every sportsman in America
and whom many of you guides
have known personally...the man who is called
the "Father of the Out-of-Doors Idea"—

W.H.H. Murray—to whom you guides
and thousands of others have lovingly given
the sobriquet he earned so well, "Adirondack Murray."

Well, as you all know, Mr. Murray's favorite guide
used to be John Plumley of Long Lake....
About two years ago,
Plumley, then an old man of seventy-four,
reached the end of the last carry....
When I learned that Plumley had passed away,
I sent word to Mr. Murray,
who I knew was planning to rejoin his old guide
here in the Adirondacks the following summer,
after an absence from this region of just twenty years;
for, when guide and sportsman had last parted
(both then in the prime of life),
a compact had been entered into between them
that if both lived to see twenty years more,
they would meet here again in the woods
the twentieth summer
and live over again their former experiences.
In the course of a few weeks Mr. Murray
sent me the following "In Memoriam" sketch
for publication in *Woods and Waters*....
I shall close these remarks with the beautiful,
pathetic eulogy which W.H.H. Murray wrote
of his oldtime guide and camp-companion,
Honest John Plumley:

"He taught me a faultless knowledge of the woods,
the name and nature of plant and herb and tree,
the languages of the night,
and the occultism of silent places and soundless shores.
I blunderingly expounded to him

the knowledge of the skies,
the names of stars, of planets and constellations
and of the splendor beyond
that was invisible as yet and would forever be
until our eyes became clearer and purer.
He had a most gentle and mannerly reticence
and that sweetest of all habits in man or woman—
the habit of silence.
He could look and see, listen and hear, and say nothing.
He was natured for reception of all fine impressions
that come to the best and the finest of the earth
out of the still depths of woods
and the quietude of far-stretching, moonlighted waters.
His knowledge of woodcraft was intuitive....
He was the only guide I ever knew of either race,
red or white, that could not in any circumstance
lose himself or his way.

"They tell me that he is dead.
It is a foolish fashion of speech and not true.
Not until the woods are destroyed to the last tree,
the mountains crumbled to their bases,
the lakes and streams dried up to their parched beds
and the woods and wood life are forgotten,
will the saying become fact.
For John Plumley was so much
of the woods, the mountains, and the streams
that he personified them.
He was a type that is deathless.
Memory, affection, imagination, literature—
until these die, the great guide of the woods will live
with ever enlarging life as the years are added to years
and the lovers of nature and of sport multiply...."
Harry V. Radford, 1903

18 ...do a common thing an uncommon way.
Booker T. Washington

I merely wish
to impress upon the great mass
of young Americans
that not only have all the great things
not been done,
but that the greatest of great things
are yet to come.

If you have greatness in you,
do not be discouraged.
It is up to you.

Do not be discouraged, either,
at failure and rebuke and defeat....

Do the thing
which is in proportion to yourself;
and if that thing is not great,
still you have served yourself,
your family,
your country,
and the world,
just as much as he
who has done a larger thing,
and you deserve
just as much credit for doing it.
Albert J. Beveridge, 1905

Everyone knows what it is
to start a piece of work,
either intellectual or muscular,
feeling stale—or *cold,*
as an Adirondack guide once put it to me.
And everybody knows what it is
to "warm up" to his job.
The process of warming up
gets particularly striking
in the phenomenon known
as "second wind."

On usual occasions
we make a practice
of stopping an occupation
as soon as we meet the first effective layer
(so to call it) of fatigue.
We have then walked,
played,
or worked "enough,"
so we desist.
That amount of fatigue
is an efficacious obstruction on this side
of which our usual life is cast.
But if unusual necessity
forces us to press onward,
a surprising thing occurs.
The fatigue gets worse
up to a certain critical point,
when gradually
or suddenly it passes away,
and we are fresher than before.

We have evidently
tapped a level of new energy,
masked till then
by the fatigue-obstacle usually obeyed.
There may be layer after layer
of this experience.
A third and a fourth "wind" may supervene.
Mental activity shows the phenomenon
as well as physical,
and in exceptional cases we may find,
beyond the very extremity of fatigue-distress,
amounts of ease and power
that we never dreamed ourselves to own,–
sources of strength
habitually not taxed at all,
because habitually
we never push through the obstruction,
never pass those early critical points.
William James, 1906

Men who have left their mark on the world
have often been implicit followers of their faith
when they could see no light,
and their faith has led them
through the wilderness of doubt and hardship
into the promised land.
Our faith often tells us
that we may proceed safely even in the dark,
when we see no light ahead.
Faith is a divine leader
which never misdirects us.
 We must only be sure that it is faith,
and not merely egotism or selfish desire.
Our faith puts us in touch with the infinite;
opens the way to unbounded possibilities,
limitless power.
It is the truth of our being.
It is the one thing
that we can be sure will not mislead us.

An unwavering belief in oneself
destroys the greatest enemies of achievement,–
fear, doubt, and vacillation.
It removes the thousand and one obstacles
which impede the progress of the weak and irresolute.
Faith in one's mission –
in the conviction that the Creator
has given us power to realize our life call,
as it is written in our blood
and stamped on our brain cells,–
is the secret of all power.
Orison Swett Marden, 1908

I who am blind
can give one hint to those who see—
one admonition to those
who would make full use of the gift of sight:
Use your eyes
as if tomorrow
you would be stricken blind.
And the same method can be applied
to the other senses.

Hear the music of voices,
the song of a bird,
the mighty strains of an orchestra,
as if you would be stricken deaf tomorrow.

Touch each object you want to touch
as if tomorrow
your tactile sense would fail.

Smell the perfume of flowers,
taste with relish each morsel,
as if tomorrow
you could never smell and taste again.

Make the most of every sense;
glory in all the facets of pleasure and beauty
which the world reveals to you
through the several means of contact
which Nature provides.
But of all the senses,
sight must be the most delightful.
Helen Keller

23 Though all else
    may be transitory in human affairs,
    the excellent
    must become the permanent.
    Jane Addams

24 The qualities
    of honesty, energy, frugality, integrity,
    are more necessary than ever to-day,
    and there is no success without them.
    They are so often urged
    that they have become commonplace,
    but they are really more prized than ever.
    And any good fortune
    that comes by such methods
    is deserved and admirable.
    Marshall Field

Is it not notorious
that one of the most marked peculiarities
of democratic society,
or of a society drifting toward democracy,
is the fire of competition
which rages in it,
the fevered anxiety
which possesses all members
to rise above the dead level
to which the law
is ever seeking to confine them,
and by some brilliant stroke
become something higher and more remarkable
than other fellows?

The secret of that great restlessness
which is one of the most
disagreeable accompaniments of life
in democratic countries,
is in fact due
to the eagerness of everybody
to grasp the prizes of which
in aristocratic countries,
only the few have such a chance.
And in no other society
is success
more worshipped,
is distinction of any kind
more widely flattered and caressed.

In democratic societies,
excellence is the first title to distinction;

in aristocratic ones
there are two or three others
which are far stronger and which must be stronger
or aristocracy could not exist.
The moment you acknowledge
that the highest social position ought to be reward
of the man who has the most talent,
you make aristocratic institutions impossible.

All that was buoyant and creative in American life
would be lost if we gave up the respect
for distinct personality,
and the variety of genius,
and came to the dead level of common standards.
To be "socialized into an average"
and placed "under the mass of us,"
would be an irreparable loss.
Frederick Jackson Turner, 1914

In every field of human endeavor,
he that is first must perpetually live
in the white light of publicity.

Whether the leadership
be vested in a man
or in a manufactured product,
emulation and envy are ever at work.

In art,
in literature,
in music,
in industry,
the reward and the punishment
are always the same.
The reward
is widespread recognition;
the punishment,
fierce denial and detraction.

When a man's work
becomes a standard for the whole world,
it also becomes a target
for the shafts of the envious few.
If his work be merely mediocre,
he will be left severely alone—
if he achieves a masterpiece,
it will set a million tongues a-wagging.

Jealousy does not protrude
its forked tongue at the artist
who produces a commonplace painting.

Whatsoever you write, or paint,
or play, or sing, or build,
no one will strive to surpass,
or to slander you,
unless your work be stamped
with the seal of genius.

Long, long after a great work
or a good work has been done,
those who are disappointed or envious
continue to cry out that it cannot be done.

Spiteful little voices
in the domain of art
were raised against
our own Whistler as a mountebank,
long after the big world had acclaimed him
its greatest artistic genius.

Multitudes flocked to Bayreuth
to worship at the musical shrine of Wagner,
while the little group of those
whom he had dethroned and displaced
argued angrily that he was no musician at all.

The little world continued to protest
that Fulton could never build a steamboat,
while the big world flocked to the river banks
to see his boat steam by.

The leader is assailed
because he is a leader,
and the effort to equal him
is merely added proof of that leadership.

Failing to equal or excel,
the follower seeks to depreciate and destroy—
but only confirms once more the superiority
of that which he strives to supplant.

There is nothing new in this.

It is as old as the world
and as old as the human passions—
envy, fear, greed, ambition,
and the desire to surpass.
And it all avails nothing.

If the leader truly leads,
he remains—
the leader.
Master-poet,
master-painter,
master-workman,
each in this turn is assailed,
and each holds his laurels through the ages.

That which is good
or great makes itself known,
no matter how loud the clamor of denial.

That which deserves to live—lives.
Theodore F. MacManus
Cadillac Motor Car Company, 1914

I believe
in the United States of America
as a government
of the people,
by the people,
for the people;
whose just powers are derived
from the consent of the governed;
a democracy in a republic;
a sovereign state
of many sovereign states;
a perfect union,
one and inseparable,
established upon those principles
of freedom, equality, justice and humanity,
for which American patriots
sacrificed their lives and fortunes.
I therefore believe
it is my duty to my country
to love it,
to support its constitution,
to obey its laws,
to respect its flag,
and to defend it against all enemies.
William Tyler Page, 1918

The maritime history of Massachusetts,
then, as distinct from that of America,
ends with the passing of the clipper.
'T was a glorious ending!
Never, in these United States,
has the brain of man conceived,
or the hand of man fashioned,
so perfect a thing as the clipper ship.
In her, the long-suppressed artistic impulse
of a practical, hard-worked race
burst into flower.
The *Flying Cloud* was our Rheims,
the *Sovereign of the Seas* our Parthenon,
the *Lightning* our Amiens;
but they were monuments carved from snow.
For a brief moment of time
they flashed their splendor around the world,
then disappeared
with the sudden completeness
of the wild pigeon.
One by one
they sailed out of Boston,
to return no more.
A tragic or mysterious end
was the final privilege of many,
favored by the gods.
Others, with lofty rig cut down
to cautious dimensions,
with glistening decks and topsides
scarred and neglected,
limped about the seas under foreign flags,
like faded beauties forced upon the street.

The master builders,
reluctant to raise barnyard fowls
where once they had reared eagles,
dropped off one by one.
Donald McKay,
dying almost in poverty after a career
that should have brought him wealth and honor,
sleeps at Newburyport
among the comrades of his young manhood.
The commonwealth,
so generous in laurel
to second-rate politicians
and third-rate soldiers,
contains no memorial line to this man
who helped to make her name immortal.
But in the elm branches over his grave
the brave west winds that he loved so well,
murmur soft versions of the tunes
they once played on the shrouds
of his glorious ships.
Samuel Eliot Morison, 1921

Greatness,
in the last analysis,
is largely bravery—
courage in escaping
from old ideas and old standards
and respectable ways of doing things.
This is one of the chief elements
in what we vaguely call capacity.
If you do not dare differ
from your associates and teachers
you will never be great
or your life sublime.
You may be happier as a result,
or you may be miserable.
Each of us is great
insofar as we perceive
and act on the infinite possibilities
which lie undiscovered
and unrecognized about us.
James Harvey Robinson

30 Thinking always ahead,
    thinking always of trying to do more,
    brings a state of mind
    in which nothing seems impossible.
    Henry Ford

In the city of Bagdad
lived Hakeem, the Wise One,
and many people went to him for counsel,
which he gave freely to all,
asking nothing in return.

There came to him a young man,
who had spent much
but got little, and said:
"Tell me, Wise One,
what shall I do to receive the most
for which I spend?"

Hakeem answered,
"A thing that is bought or sold
has no value unless it contains that
which cannot be bought or sold.
Look for the Priceless Ingredient."

"But, what is this Priceless Ingredient?"
asked the young man.

Spoke then the Wise One,
"My son, the Priceless Ingredient
of every product in the marketplace
is the Honor and Integrity
of him who makes it.
Consider his name before you buy."
E.R. Squibb & Sons, 1921

Whose woods these are I think I know.
His house is in the village though;
He will not see me stopping here
To watch his woods fill up with snow.

My little horse must think it queer
To stop without a farmhouse near
Between the woods and frozen lake
The darkest evening of the year.

He gives his harness bells a shake
To ask if there is some mistake.
The only other sound's the sweep
Of easy wind and downy flake.

The woods are lovely, dark and deep.
But I have promises to keep,
And miles to go before I sleep,
And miles to go before I sleep.
Robert Frost, 1923

On the night of August 2, 1923,
I was awakened
by my father coming up the stairs,
calling my name.
I noticed that his voice trembled.
As the only times
I had ever observed that before were
when death had visited our family,
I knew that something
of the gravest nature had occurred.

His emotion was partly due to the knowledge
that a man whom he had met and liked
was gone, partly to the feeling
that must possess all of our citizens
when the life of their President
is taken from them.

But he must have been moved
also by the thought
of the many sacrifices he had made
to place me where I was,
the twenty-five mile drives in storms
and zero weather over our mountain roads
to carry me to the academy,
and all the tenderness and care
he had lavished upon me
in the thirty-eight years
since the death of my mother,
in the hope that I might sometime rise
to a position of importance,
which he now saw realized.

He was now the first to address me
as President of the United States.
It was a culmination
of the lifelong desire of a father
for the success of his son.

He placed in my hands
an official report and told me
that President Harding had just passed away...
Calvin Coolidge, 1923

Not only as folk but as individual artists
the Negro in America is a creator;
and as such,
he has exercised an influence
greater than it is yet realized to be,
and which is far in excess
of what his numbers and status
would seem to warrant.

There is one other contribution
the Negro in America has made
that will eventually influence national thought.
I hesitate to stress it
because it is so intangible.
However, it is the contribution in spiritual values
that he has made through the fortitude
with which he has borne himself
and steadily forced his way forward.
James Weldon Johnson

35 Still—
in a way—
nobody sees a flower—
really—
it is so small—
we haven't time—
and to see takes time,
like to have a friend takes time.
Georgia O'Keeffe

There is little importance to men's lives
except the accomplishments
they leave to posterity.
What a man accomplishes is
of many categories
and of many points of view;
moral influence,
example,
leadership in thought
and inspiration
are difficult to measure,
to prove or to treasure...
and the proportion of success
to be attributed to their effort
is always indeterminate.
In the origination or administration
of tangible institutions or constructive works
men's parts can be more certainly defined.
When all is said and done
accomplishment is all that counts.
Record of failure may be warning,
guiding information or vicarious sacrifice,
but it [is] the progress marched that counts,
not the description of the road
or the conversation and gossip.
Herbert Hoover

37   The toughest thing about success is
     that you've got to keep on being a success.
     Irving Berlin

Chug, chug, chug.
Puff, puff, puff.
Ding-dong, ding-dong.
The little train rumbled over the tracks.
She was a happy little train
for she had such a jolly load to carry.
Her cars were full
of good things for boys and girls.

There were toy animals—
giraffes with long necks,
teddy bears with almost no necks at all,
and even a baby elephant.
Then there were dolls—
dolls with blue eyes and yellow curls,
dolls with brown eyes and brown bobbed heads,
and the funniest little toy clown
you ever saw.
And there were cars full
of toy engines, airplanes, tops,
jack-knives, picture puzzles, books,
and every kind of thing boys or girls could want.

But that was not all.
Some of the cars
were filled with all sorts of good things
for boys and girls to eat—
big golden oranges, red-cheeked apples,
bottles of creamy milk for their breakfasts,
fresh spinach for their dinners,
peppermint drops,
and lollypops for after-meal treats.

The little train
was carrying all these wonderful things
to the good little boys and girls
on the other side of the mountain.
She puffed along merrily.
Then all of a sudden she stopped with a jerk.
She simply could not go another inch.
She tried and she tried,
but her wheels would not turn.

What were all those good little boys and girls
on the other side of the mountain going to do
without the wonderful toys to play with
and the good food to eat?

"Here comes a shiny new engine,"
said the funny little clown
who jumped out of the train,
"Let us ask him to help us."

So all the dolls and toys cried out together:
"Please, Shiny New Engine,
won't you please
pull our train over the mountain?
Our engine has broken down,
and the boys and girls on the other side
won't have any toys to play with
or good food to eat unless you help us."

But the Shiny New Engine snorted:
"I pull you? I am a Passenger Engine.
I have just carried a fine big train
over the mountain,
with more cars than you ever dreamed of.

My train had sleeping cars,
with comfortable berths;
a dining-car where waiters
bring whatever hungry people want to eat;
and parlor cars in which people
sit in arm-chairs and look out
of big plate-glass windows.
I pull the likes of you?
Indeed not!"
And off he steamed to the roundhouse,
where engines live when they are not busy.

How sad the little train
and all the dolls and toys felt!
Then the little clown called out,
"The Passenger Engine is not the only one in the world.
Here is another engine coming,
a great big strong one.
Let us ask him to help us."

The little toy clown waved his flag
and the big strong engine came to a stop.

"Please, oh, please, Big Engine,"
cried all the dolls and toys together.
"Won't you please
pull our train over the mountain?
Our engine has broken down,
and the good little boys and girls on the other side
won't have any toys to play with
or good food to eat unless you help us."

But the Big Strong Engine bellowed:
"I am a Freight Engine.

I have just pulled a big train
loaded with big machines over the mountain.
These machines print books and newspapers
for grown-ups to read.
I am a very important engine indeed.
I won't pull the likes of you!"
And the Freight Engine
pulled off indignantly to the roundhouse.

The little train
and all the dolls and toys were very sad.

"Cheer up,"
cried the little toy clown.
"The Freight Engine is not the only one in the world.
Here comes another.
He looks very old and tired,
but our train is so little,
perhaps he can help us."

So the little toy clown waved his flag
and the dingy, rusty old engine stopped.

"Please, Kind Engine,"
cried all the dolls and toys together.
"Won't you please
pull our train over the mountain?
Our engine has broken down,
and the boys and girls on the other side
won't have any toys to play with
or good food to eat unless you help us."

But the Rusty Old Engine sighed:
"I am so tired.

I must rest my weary wheels.
I cannot pull even so little a train as yours
over the mountain.
I can not. I can not. I can not."

And off he rumbled to the roundhouse chugging,
" I can not. I can not. I can not."

Then indeed the little train
was very, very sad,
and the dolls and toys were ready to cry.

But the little clown called out,
" Here is another engine coming,
a little blue engine, a very little one,
maybe she will help us."

The very little engine
came chug, chugging merrily along.
When she saw the toy clown's flag,
she stopped quickly.

"What is the matter, my friends?"
she asked kindly.

" Oh, Little Blue Engine,"
cried the dolls and toys.
"Will you pull us over the mountain?
Our engine has broken down
and the good boys and girls on the other side
won't have any toys to play with
or good food to eat, unless you help us.
Please, please, help us,
Little Blue Engine."

" I'm not very big,"
  said the Little Blue Engine.
"They use me only for switching trains in the yard.
  I have never been over the mountain."

" But we must get over the mountain
  before the children awake,"
  said all the dolls and toys.

  The very little engine looked up
  and saw the tears in the dolls' eyes.
  And she thought of the good little boys and girls
  on the other side of the mountain
  who would not have any toys or food unless she helped.

  Then she said,
"I think I can.
  I think I can.
  I think I can."
  And she hitched herself to the little train.

  She tugged and pulled and pulled and tugged
  and slowly, slowly, slowly they started off.

  The toy clown jumped aboard
  and all the dolls and the toy animals
  began to smile and cheer.

  Puff, puff, chug, chug,
  went the Little Blue Engine.
"I think I can—
  I think I can—
  I think I can—
  I think I can—

I think I can—
I think I can—
I think I can—
I think I can—
I think I can."

Up, up, up.
Faster and faster and faster and faster
the little engine climbed,
until at last
they reached the top of the mountain.

Down in the valley lay the city.

"Hurray, hurray,"
cried the funny little clown
and all the dolls and toys.
"The good little boys and girls in the city
will be happy because you helped us,
kind, Little Blue Engine."

And the Little Blue Engine smiled
and seemed to say
as she puffed steadily down the mountain:
"I thought I could.
I thought I could.
I thought I could.
I thought I could.
I thought I could.
I thought I could."
Retold by Watty Piper, 1930

39 So live
    that you wouldn't be ashamed
    to sell the family parrot
    to the town gossip.
    Will Rogers

I don't know anything about selling automobiles;
I never sold one in my life; but perhaps
a few remarks here on the psychology
that is necessary for success
in a football organization
might not be out of place,
because it seems to me that the same psychology
that makes for success in a football organization
will make for success in any organization,
particularly in a selling organization.

Now, in the fall
when we make our first call for the team,
for the lads to come out,
about three hundred and fifty of them assemble
in a large room in the library
somewhat like this one;
and it is my idea to talk to them
on the correct psychology
before I take them out on the field.
I talk to them on ambition
and I tell them that most
of that which I read about ambition is bunk.
There is not plenty of room at the top.
There is very little room at the top.
There is room at the top only for the few
who have the ability,
the imagination, the daring,
the personality, and the energy
that make them stand out from their fellow-men.
But there is success for any man in his own job
if he does as well as it can be done.

As far as I am able to observe,
the greatest satisfaction
I can get on this earth
is to do the particular job I am doing
as well as it can be done;
and I think that holds good for anyone.
There may be other things that are easier,
but they generally leave a headache
or a heartache the day after.

I tell the lads there are six types
that I do not want.
The first type I have in mind
is the swelled head,
the man who was a success a year ago,
who is content to rest on his laurels,
who wants to play on his reputation.
Dry rot sets in,
and he ceases to make an effort.
To that kind of boy
there will come quite a shock,
because the chances are
there will be someone playing in his place.

The second type of lad
is the chronic complainer.
He crabs everyone but himself.
And I say no organization
can afford to have that type of man,
because he is infectious.
He is in for a shock, too,
because as soon as I find out who he is,
some day when he comes out for practice—
there will be no suit in his locker.

And third is the quitter.
The quitter is the fellow who wishes he could play,
but is not willing to pay the price.
And I tell the boys if any of that type is there,
he might just as well quit then
and not wear out the equipment.

Fourth, I don't want boys to dissipate,
physically or emotionally.
I tell them that I hold no brief against
playing pool long hours in the afternoon,
dancing half the night,
or learning to drive an automobile with one hand;
but I tell them
that they have no time for it.
If they are going
to compete with organizations
which do not do that sort of thing
and which are saving all their energy
for the contest, I say,
they should not dissipate any energy emotionally.
And by that I mean
that they should not give way to emotions
such as jealousy, hatred,
or anything of that sort.
That sort of thing destroys any organization.

And then I tell them
that they should look upon one another
in a friendly way,
look for the good in one another,
and be inspired by the fine qualities
in those around them
and forget about their faults.

I tell them that the chances are
that I will notice the faults—
and won't stutter when I mention them
to the particular individual who has them.
The man who lacks friendliness is the fifth.

There is a sixth type of undesirable;
he suffers from an inferiority complex.
He generally comes
from a small community
and he says to himself,
"What chances have I got
to get on the first string
of thirty-three men here, when there are
three hundred and fifty boys trying out for it?
I don't believe I've got a chance;
I don't believe I can make it."
"If there are any among you," I say,
"who feel that way, forget about it,
and get a superiority complex.
You are just as good as any man out here.
And by getting a superiority complex
you can show the coach you belong
at the top of the thirty-three men
where you would like to be."

I remember about four years ago
I divided the men on the field into groups—
the ends, tackles, guards, centers,
quarter-backs, and so forth.
I walked to the group of guards.
Now, guard is a position
demanding a certain amount
of physical ruggedness.

There were fifteen
good-sized boys in the group
and one little chap
whose name was Metzger.
I said to him,
"Aren't you a little slight
and small to be playing guard?"
"Yes," he answered, "but I'm a little rough."
That confidence enabled him last fall,
in spite of the fact
that he weighed only 149 pounds,
to hold his own against any opponent
whether he weighed 200 pounds or more.

In two weeks I call them together again
and I tell them that there are certain among them
that have great potentialities,
but that they have not shown any improvement.
There are certain ones among them
that I do not want unless they change.

The first is the chap who alibis,
who justifies his own failure.
And I tell them that a boy
who does this had better watch out
or he will get into another class,
that of feeling sorry for himself,
in which case the bony part of his spine
turns into a soft colloidal substance known as "soap,"
and he is absolutely worthless.

The second class of lad—
I generally have very few of them—
is the slicker, the mucker, who tries to get by

by playing unfair football.
And I tell that type of boy
that we cannot afford to have him on the team,
for he will bring discredit on the school
and on our organization.
I also impress on him
that slugging and unfairness do not pay,
either in a game or in life after leaving school.

Then, third, there is the boy
who lacks courage, who is afraid.
What is courage?
Courage means
to be afraid to do something
but still to go ahead and do it.
If a man has character,
the right kind of energy and mental ability,
he will learn that fear is something to overcome
and not to run away from.

Before the first game of the year
I talk to them again on ambition.
I say ambition,
the right kind of ambition,
means the ability to cooperate
with the men around them,
men who are working with them.
It is my observation
that ability to cooperate
is more essential
than individual technique.
In this day
no individual stands alone any more;
he must cooperate in every sense of the word:

and that is not a very easy thing to do in football,
because in our colleges
we often get boys who have been spoiled
by the local press in their high school days.
They kick the ball well,
pass pretty well,
and once in a while they run with it.
They are all pretty good.
If you don't believe it, they have clippings
along with them to prove it.
Teaching cooperation
is not always the easiest thing
in the world,
especially to a group of boys....

In any organization
no one man
can enjoy the spotlight all the time
while the rest of the boys are doing the chores.
Each one has to take his turn doing the chores.

I began the practice
of putting up signs in the locker rooms
where the boys had to read them.
I put up a half dozen signs, figuring
that would impress certain things on their minds.
One sign which applied in this particular case read
"Success is based on what the team does,
not on how you look."
The result is I have had little trouble
along that line since,
although now and then
I may have to hang up that sign
in an individual locker.

And when I do,
the boy brings the sign back to me
and says,
"You got me all wrong, Coach."
And I say,
"Was that hanging in your locker?
Oh, I beg your pardon."
But it has its effect just the same.

Later on after a game or two,
and particularly after a game
where I have seen the lads give up,
I talk to them further on ambition.
I tell them that there can be
no ambition without perseverance.
By perseverance
I mean the ability to stick in there
and keep giving the best of one's self.
There can be no success, no reward,
unless every man has the ability to stay in there
until the last whistle blows.

I was down in New York a few years ago;
and in the company
of Lawrence Perry, the author,
I visited the Players' Club.
He was showing me through the club
and was telling me
about its being founded by Booth,
the famous Shakespearean actor,
and how Booth was the first president,
and how under his guidance
the club had always maintained
a very fine high standard of membership.

As we were going through,
we came to a room
where there was a table and chair,
and Perry told me
that Booth was wont to go there,
when he was tired,
to read and study.
One afternoon
while sitting and reading,
he died.
The table and chair
were left in the same place
in memory of Booth,
and the book
has been left open at the very place
where he was reading at the time he passed away.
Out of curiosity, I stepped up
to find out what he had been reading
at that particular moment.
It was Pope's *Essay on Man*.
You all remember it.
The first line reads —
"Hope springs eternal in the human breast."
Glancing quickly down the page
I read the last line. It said,
"But if hope eludes you, all is lost."

Going back to Notre Dame,
I carried that message to the boys.
I talked to them about it,
until I felt that every one of them
was thoroughly imbued with that psychology.
That year our last game
was with Southern California in Los Angeles.

With but seven or eight minutes to play
we were ahead seven to six.
I, of course, thought
the game was pretty well over,
and felt that the one point lead we had
was sufficient to win;
but just then the Southern California boys
began to collect themselves
and started an irresistible drive down the field.
I changed my guards, tackles;
but still on they came,
three and four yards at a time,
over our goal line for a touchdown.
And although they missed the goal,
that made the score twelve to seven
in favor of Southern California
with about three minutes to play.
"Well," I said,
" I guess it is all over but the shouting."

We elected to receive the kick-off,
and brought the ball
back to the twenty yard line.
Here we tried three plays
without making an inch;
so, finally, on the fourth down,
kicked down the field to Southern California,
who punted the ball right back,
as if to say,
"There it is; what are you going to do with it?"
We had seventy yards to go.
In those three plays on the twenty yard line
I had seen something
I had hoped I wouldn't see.

I saw ten men still doggedly trying
for all they were worth;
but the eleventh lad,
a little third-string quarter-back was through.
As far as he was concerned, the game was over.
Hope had eluded him.
I don't blame him,
for he was just a normal young lad
nineteen years old.
I turned around to a little chap
sitting behind me on the bench,
who had been injured earlier in the season
and had not played much,
little Art Parisien; and I said,
"Art, how do you feel?
Do you think if I put you in there
you can pull old 83 and 84,
those left-handed passes of yours,
and maybe still pull the game out of the fire?"
Before I had finished talking,
he had his head-gear on and was already on the field.
As he was leaving,
he turned around and hollered back to me,
"Coach, it's a cinch."

That may sound like egotism, but it wasn't.
A man once defined egotism to me as
"the anaesthetic that deadens the pain of one's stupidity."
You can be assured that
that was not the case with this lad.
He felt that he could do it,
for he had done it
just a short time previously
against Northwestern in Chicago.

He felt that he could do it,
because he was filled with hope.
On the first play he pulled a play
of nine yards straight through the line,
after which he called time out.
Then he called those ten lads around him
(for he could not talk to them
until after the first play),
and you could see him
imbuing them with his optimism.
He lifted those ten team-mates of his;
and to my surprise, they lined up
and did pull old 83, that left-handed pass,
which was good for a gain of twenty-three yards.
I thought that was fine,
but I still didn't see how we had a chance.
There were now left
only two minutes and a quarter to play.
Next he pulled a side-end run
to the right side of the field for position,
and there was less than a minute to play.
Then he pulled old 84,
that left-handed pass to a lad named Niemic,
who went over for the winning touchdown.
Winning the game is not important,
although interesting.
The important thing to me
was the fact
that this team wouldn't be beaten,
and proved to me that the team,
or the individual,
that *will not* be beaten *can not* be beaten.
Knute K. Rockne, 1931

When Hurley's wife telephoned me
that he was desperately ill with pneumonia
I was preparing to sail for Europe within the hour,
but I dropped everything to hasten to his bedside.
I had been Hurley's roommate at college
and best man at his wedding,
and although I had not seen him for several years
the warmth of our friendship persisted.

As I taxied posthaste to the hospital
I carried with me the mental picture
of the same unchanging Hurley I had always known—
an undersized, mild-mannered type of man,
hesitant and undecided as to character,
now nearing forty, and apparently
reconciled to remain forever a plodding clerk.

But the moment I glimpsed him
I was conscious of a startling change.
Hurley had been somehow transformed
into an entirely different type of person,
and solely through the alchemy of a smile.

It was not the resigned smile
of one reconciled to death.
It was a smile of victory,
of proud achievement, of triumphant success—
things never even remotely associated with Hurley.

"I've won," he breathed.
"I've won at last.
Thank God I'm a success."

Through the delirium
of intermittent unconsciousness
Hurley's declaration of victory and success
was repeated again and again.

The nurse, sharing my startled wonderment,
whisperingly confided the details.
At the time of the attending physician's diagnosis
they had thought Hurley asleep,
only to discover that he had overheard
the tragically brief remark of the physician—
a few ominous words
virtually sealing Hurley's doom.
And it was upon hearing these words
that Hurley had first smiled his smile of success.

To add to our bewilderment
we knew that Hurley wanted to live.
Among many other reasons
was the bond between him and his wife,
a colorless, repressed little woman
who moved meekly in an aura of self-obliteration,
and who seemed a perfect complement
to Hurley's mild negations of character.
Between them was a deep love,
a piteous, clinging-together type of devotion
which had always been woven
through the drab texture of their lives.

She was sitting there at his bedside,
tremulously whispering words
of endearment and encouragement to him.
The pressing proximity of my sailing hour
drew me reluctantly from the room.

As I paused at the door
for a last lingering look at my friend,
there came once more Hurley's exultant tocsin:

"I've won; I'm a success."

And accompanying the words
was the illuminating glory of his triumphant smile —
a smile born in the same moment
that he had heard
the sentence of death passed upon him.

I was well out at sea
when the agony of my suspenseful waiting
was finally relieved by the arrival of a radiogram.
I opened it tremblingly.
Hurley had passed the crisis and would live!....

Business kept me in Europe for more than a year.
Almost immediately upon my return home
a telephone message from Hurley
took me to his office.
If I had been amazed at the metamorphosis
of the man at the hospital,
I was dumbfounded now.
Hurley, radiant with success,
was established in a splendidly appointed office,
the enthusiastic head of a flourishing brokerage business.

He immediately sensed my profound bewilderment,
chuckled delightedly,
settled back in his chair,
and told me his story —
the story of "Half-Way" Hurley.

He began with his entrance into matrimony,
only half-way prepared for its responsibilities.
He dwelt at length
upon his half-way success as an accountant;
of half-way health;
of the half-paid mortgage upon his home,
a home which was bereft of children
because Hurley felt himself only half-way fitted
for the exactions of parenthood.

"And so I drifted on and on,"
  he explained,
"always at the half-way mark in everything,
  until my inner mind
  was dominated by the psychology of defeatism,
  and my subconscious self
  labeled me 'Half-Way' Hurley.

"Finally I began to grow ashamed of myself.
  I thought of my wife.
  I began to want success.
  Desperately I began to plan success.
  I knew that I was a victim of psychology,
  and I knew that the laws of psychology work both ways.
  I reasoned
  that if there could be one thing in my life
  not done half-way
  that thing would serve
  as a psychological symbol of success.

"On the spur of the moment I selected
  my half-completed garden as that symbol.
  I worked furiously,
  trying to rush it to a completed condition.

I badly overtaxed my strength
and in a moment of lowered resistance
contracted my pneumonia.
I was carried to the hospital
bitter with the realization
that I was still 'Half-Way' Hurley—
that I still lacked my symbol of success.
Man, how I wanted that symbol of one thing well done.
How I needed it!

"And then, suddenly,
the physician who examined me
gave that symbol with words
never intended for my ears—
words which virtually portended my death
but which, ironically and whimsically enough,
were to me the elixir of life;
words which gave birth to my smile of achievement;
words which made me resolve not only to live,
but to push everything in my future life
to completion and success.
They were the words spoken by the doctor
to the nurse when he said:
'There's nothing half-way about this case;
he has *double* pneumonia.'

"And there was my symbol.
At last I had stopped doing things by halves."
In the silence that followed,
Hurley's telephone rang
and I heard him conversing with his wife.
And in those few sentences
was tenderly crystallized all of the love
one human can bear for another.

"This time it's my wife who is in the hospital,"
   Hurley said as he hung up.
" I've got to hustle over there at once
   and you must come along.
   You see, that's the real reason I've sent for you.
   There's to be an addition to the family
   and you're to be godfather."

   Enthusiastically I shouted my congratulations,
   and asked:
"What is it—a girl or a boy?"

   Hurley threw back his head
   with a long joyous laugh—
   a laugh vibrant with the pride
   and strength and power
   that comes with assured success.

"There's nothing half-way about that, either,"
   he exulted.
"It's both!"
   Dr. George Crane, 1931

About a year and a half ago
a young man came to the front door
of the house in Key West
and said that he had hitch-hiked down
from upper Minnesota
to ask your correspondent
a few questions about writing.
Arrived that day from Cuba,
having to see some good friends off
on the train in an hour,
and to write some letters in the meantime,
your correspondent, both flattered and appalled
at the prospect of the questioning,
told the young man
to come around the next afternoon.
He was a tall, very serious young man
with very big feet and hands
and a porcupine hair-cut.

It seemed that all his life
he had wanted to be a writer.
Brought up on a farm
he had gone through high school
and the University of Minnesota,
had worked as a newspaper man,
a rough carpenter, a harvest hand, a day laborer,
and had bummed his way across America twice.
He wanted to be a writer
and he had good stories to write.
He told them very badly but you could see
that there was something there
if he could get it out.

He was so entirely serious about writing
that it seemed that seriousness
would overcome all obstacles.
He had lived by himself for a year
in a cabin he had built in North Dakota
and written all that year.
He did not show me anything
that he had written then.
It was all bad, he said.

I thought, perhaps, that this was modesty
until he showed me a piece he had published
in one of the Minneapolis papers.
It was abominably written.
Still, I thought,
many other people write badly at the start
and this boy is so extremely serious
that he must have something;
real seriousness in regard to writing
being one of the two absolute necessities.
The other, unfortunately, is talent.
Besides writing
this young man had one other obsession.
He had always wanted to go to sea.
So, to shorten this account, we gave him a job
as night watchman on the boat
which furnished him a place to sleep and work
and gave him two or three hours' work
each day at cleaning up
and a half of each day free
to do his writing.
To fulfill his desire to go to sea,
we promised to take him to Cuba
when we went across.

He was an excellent night watchman
and worked hard on the boat and at his writing
but at sea he was a calamity;
slow where he should be agile,
seeming sometimes to have four feet
instead of two feet and two hands,
nervous under excitement,
and with an incurable tendency toward sea-sickness
and a peasant reluctance to take orders.
Yet he was always willing and hard working
if given plenty of time to work in.

We called him the Maestro because he played the violin,
this name was eventually shortened to the Mice,
and a big breeze
would so effectually slow up his co-ordination
that your correspondent once remarked to him,
"Mice, you certainly must be going to be
a hell of a good writer because you certainly
aren't worth a damn at anything else."

On the other hand his writing improved steadily.
He may yet be a writer. But your correspondent,
who sometimes has an evil temper,
is never going to ship another hand
who is an aspirant writer;
nor go through another summer
off the Cuban or any other coast
accompanied by questions and answers
on the practice of letters.
If any more aspirant writers
come on board the *Pilar* let them be females,
let them be very beautiful,
and let them bring champagne.

Your correspondent
takes the practice of letters,
as distinct from the writing
of these monthly letters, very seriously;
but dislikes intensely talking about it
with almost anyone alive.
Having had to mouth about many aspects of it
during a period of one hundred and ten days
with the good old Maestro,
during much of which time
your correspondent
had to conquer an urge
to throw a bottle at the Mice
whenever he would open his mouth
and pronounce the word writing,
he hereby presents
some of these mouthings written down.

If they can deter anyone from writing
he should be deterred.
If they can be of use to anyone
your correspondent is pleased.
If they bore you
there are plenty of pictures in the magazine
that you may turn to.

Your correspondent's excuse
for presenting them is
that some of the information contained
would have been worth fifty cents to him
when he was twenty-one.

Mice: What do you mean by good writing
as opposed to bad writing?

Your correspondent:
Good writing is true writing.
If a man is making a story up
it will be true in proportion to the amount
of knowledge of life that he has
and how conscientious he is;
so that when he makes something up
it is as it would truly be.
If he doesn't know how many people
work in their minds and actions
his luck may save him for a while,
or he may write fantasy.
But if he continues to write about
what he does not know about
he will find himself faking.
After he fakes a few times
he cannot write honestly any more.

Mice: Then what about imagination?

Y.C.:   Nobody knows a damned thing about it
except that it is what we get for nothing.
It may be racial experience.
I think that is quite possible.
It is the one thing beside honesty
that a good writer must have.
The more he learns from experience
the more truly he can imagine.
If he gets so he can imagine
truly enough people will think
that the things he relates all really happened
and that he is just reporting.

Mice: Where will it differ from reporting?

Y.C.:   If it was reporting
they would not remember it.
When you describe something
that has happened that day
the timeliness makes people see it
in their own imaginations.
A month later
that element of time is gone
and your account would be flat
and they would not see it in their minds
nor remember it.
But if you make it up
instead of describe it
you can make it round and whole
and solid and give it life.
You create it, for good or bad.
It is made; not described.
It is just as true
as the extent of your ability to make it
and the knowledge you put into it.
Do you follow me?

Mice: Not always.

Y.C.:   Well for chrisake let's talk
about something else then.

Mice: Tell me some more
about the mechanics of writing.

Y.C.:   What do you mean?
Like pencil or typewriter? For chrisake.

Mice: Yes.

Y.C.:   Listen. When you start to write
you get all the kick and the reader gets none.
So you might as well use a typewriter
because it is that much easier
and you enjoy it that much more.
After you learn to write
your whole object is to convey everything,
every sensation, sight, feeling, place
and emotion to the reader.
To do this you have to work over what you write.
If you write with a pencil
you get three different sights at it
to see if the reader is getting
what you want him to.
First when you read it over;
then when it is typed
you get another chance to improve it,
and again in the proof.
Writing it first in pencil
gives you one-third more chance
to improve it. That is .333
which is a damned good average for a hitter.
It also keeps it fluid longer
so that you can better it easier.

Mice: How much should you write a day?

Y.C.:   The best way is always to stop
when you are going good
and when you know what will happen next.
If you do that every day when you are writing a novel
you will never be stuck.
That is the most valuable thing I can tell you
so try to remember it.

Mice: All right.

Y.C.:   Always stop while you are going good
        and don't think about it or worry about it
        until you start to write the next day.
        That way your subconscious
        will work on it all the time.
        But if you think about it consciously
        or worry about it you will kill it
        and your brain will be tired before you start.
        Once you are into the novel
        it is as cowardly to worry about
        whether you can go on the next day
        as to worry about
        having to go into inevitable action.
        You *have* to go on.
        So there is no sense to worry.
        You have to learn that to write a novel.
        The hard part about a novel is to finish it.

Mice: How can you learn not to worry?

Y.C.:   By not thinking about it.
        As soon as you start to think about it stop it.
        Think about something else.
        You have to learn that.

Mice: How much do you read over every day
        before you start to write?

Y.C.:   The best way is to read it all
        every day from the start,
        correcting as you go along, then go on
        from where you stopped the day before.

When it gets so long
that you can't do this every day
read back two or three chapters each day;
then each week read it all from the start.
That's how you make it all of one piece.
And remember to stop
while you are still going good.
That keeps it moving
instead of having it die
whenever you go on and write yourself out.
When you do that
you find that the next day
you are pooped and can't go on.

Mice: Do you do the same on a story?

Y.C.:   Yes, only sometimes you can write a story in a day.

Mice: Do you know what is going to happen
        when you write a story?

Y.C.:   Almost never.
        I start to make it up and have happen
        what would have to happen as it goes along.

Mice: That isn't the way
        they teach you to write in college.

Y.C.:   I don't know about that.
        I never went to college.
        If any sonofabitch could write
        he wouldn't have to teach writing in college.

Mice: You're teaching me.

Y.C.: I'm crazy.
Besides this is a boat, not a college.

Mice: What books should a writer have to read?

Y.C.: He should have read everything
so he knows what he has to beat.

Mice: He can't have read everything.

Y.C.: I don't say what he can.
I say what he should.
Of course he can't.

Mice: Well what books are necessary?

Y.C.: He should have read
War and Peace
and *Anna Karenina* by Tolstoi,
Midshipman Easy, Frank Mildmay
and *Peter Simple* by Captain Marryat,
Madame Bovary
and *L'Education Sentimentale* by Flaubert,
Buddenbrooks by Thomas Mann,
Joyce's *Dubliners,*
Portrait of the Artist and *Ulysses,*
Tom Jones and *Joseph Andrews* by Fielding.
Le Rouge et le Noir and
La Chartreuse de Parme by Stendhal,
The Brothers Karamazov
and any two other Dostoevskis,
Huckleberry Finn by Mark Twain,
The Open Boat
and *The Blue Hotel* by Stephen Crane,

Hail and Farewell by George Moore,
Yeats's *Autobiographies*,
all the good De Maupassant,
all the good Kipling,
all of Turgenev,
Far Away and Long Ago by W.H. Hudson,
Henry James's short stories,
especially *Madame de Mauves*,
and *The Turn of the Screw*,
The Portrait of a Lady, The American—

Mice: I can't write them down that fast.
How many more are there?

Y.C.:   I'll give you the rest another day.
There are about three times that many.

Mice: Should a writer have read all those?

Y.C.:   All of those and plenty more.
Otherwise he doesn't know what he has to beat.

Mice: What do you mean "has to beat"?

Y.C.:   Listen. There is no use writing anything
that has been written before unless you can beat it.
What a writer in our time has to do
is write what hasn't been written before
or beat dead men at what they have done.
The only way he can tell how he is going
is to compete with dead men.
Most live writers do not exist.
Their fame is created by critics
who always need a genius of the season,

someone they understand completely
and feel safe in praising,
but when these fabricated geniuses are dead
they will not exist.
The only people
for a serious writer to compete with
are the dead that he knows are good.
It is like a miler running against the clock
rather than simply trying to beat
whoever is in the race with him.
Unless he runs against time
he will never know
what he is capable of attaining.

Mice: But reading all the good writers
might discourage you.

Y.C.: Then you ought to be discouraged.

Mice: What is the best early training for a writer?

Y.C.: An unhappy childhood.

Mice: Do you think Thomas Mann is a great writer?

Y.C.: He would be a great writer
if he had never written another thing
than *Buddenbrooks*.

Mice: How can a writer train himself?

Y.C.: Watch what happens today.
If we get into a fish
see exactly what it is that everyone does.

If you get a kick out of it
while he is jumping
remember back
until you see exactly what the action was
that gave you the emotion.
Whether it was the rising of the line from the water
and the way it tightened like a fiddle string
until drops started from it,
or the way he smashed
and threw water when he jumped.
Remember what the noises were
and what was said.
Find what gave you the emotion;
what the action was that gave you the excitement.
Then write it down
making it clear so the reader will see it too
and have the same feeling that you had.
That's a five finger exercise.

Mice: All right.

Y.C.:   Then get in somebody else's head
for a change.
If I bawl you out
try to figure what I'm thinking about
as well as how you feel about it.
If Carlos curses Juan
think what both their sides of it are.
Don't just think who is right.
As a man things are as they should or shouldn't be.
As a man you know who is right and who is wrong.
You have to make decisions and enforce them.
As a writer you should not judge.
You should understand.

Mice: All right.

Y.C.: Listen *now*. When people talk listen completely.
Don't be thinking what you're going to say.
Most people never listen. Nor do they observe.
You should be able to go into a room
and when you come out know everything
that you saw there and not only that.
If that room gave you any feeling
you should know exactly what it was
that gave you that feeling. Try that for practice.
When you're in town stand outside the theatre
and see how the people differ
in the way they get out of taxis or motor cars.
There are a thousand ways to practice.
And always think of other people.

Mice: Do you think I will be a writer?

Y.C.: How the the hell should I know?
Maybe you have no talent.
Maybe you can't feel for other people.
You've got some good stories if you can write them.

Mice: How can I tell?

Y.C.: Write.
If you work at it five years
and you find you're no good
you can just as well shoot yourself then as now.

Mice: I wouldn't shoot myself.

Y.C.: Come around then and I'll shoot you.

Mice: Thanks.

Y.C.:   Perfectly welcome, Mice.
Now should we talk about something else?

Mice: What else?

Y.C.:   Anything else, Mice, old timer, anything else at all.

Mice: All right. But—

Y.C.:   No but. Finish. Talk about writing finish. No more.
All gone for today. Store all close up. Boss he go home.

Mice: All right then.
But tomorrow I've got some things to ask you.

Y.C.:   I'll bet you'll have fun writing
after you know just how it's done.

Mice: What do you mean?

Y.C.:   You know. Fun. Good times. Jolly.
Dashing off an old masterpiece.

Mice: Tell me—

Y.C.:   Stop it.

Mice: All right. But tomorrow—

Y.C.:   Yes, all right. Sure. But tomorrow.
Ernest Hemingway, 1935

43 All things are possible
until they are proved impossible —
and even the impossible
may be only so, as of now.
Pearl S. Buck

Charles Schwab had a mill manager
whose men weren't producing their quota of work.
"How is it,"
  Schwab asked,
"that a man as capable as you
  can't make this mill turn out what it should?"

"I don't know,"
  the man replied,
"I've coaxed the men;
  I've pushed them;
  I've sworn and cussed;
  I've threatened them
  with damnation and being fired.
  But nothing works.
  They just won't produce."

It happened to be the end of the day,
  just before the night shift came on.
"Give me a piece of chalk,"
  Schwab said.
  Then, turning to the nearest man:
"How many heats did your shift make to-day?"
"Six."

Without another word,
  Schwab chalked a big figure six on the floor,
  and walked away.
  When the night shift came in,
  they saw the six and asked what it meant.
"The big boss was in here to-day,"
  the day men said.

"He asked us how many heats we made,
 and we told him six.
 He chalked it down on the floor."

The next morning
 Schwab walked through the mill again.
 The night shift had rubbed out the six,
 and replaced it with a big seven.
 When the day shift
 reported for work the next morning,
 they saw a big seven chalked on the floor.
 So the night shift thought they were better
 than the day shift, did they?
 Well, they would show the night shift a thing or two.
 They pitched in with enthusiasm
 and when they quit that night,
 they left behind them an enormous, swaggering ten.
 Things were stepping up.
 Shortly this mill,
 that had been lagging way behind in production,
 was turning out more work
 than any other mill in the plant.

The principle?
 Let Charles Schwab say it in his own words.
"The way to get things done,
 is to stimulate competition.
 I do not mean in a sordid, money-getting way,
 but in the desire to excel."

The desire to excel!
 The challenge! Throwing down the gauntlet!
 An infallible way of appealing to men of spirit.
 Dale Carnegie, 1936

Belief in equality is an element
of the democratic credo.
It is not, however,
belief in equality of natural endowments.

Those who proclaimed
the idea of equality
did not suppose they were enunciating
a psychological doctrine,
but a legal and political one.

All individuals are entitled to equality
of treatment by law
and in its administration.

Each one is affected equally
in quality
if not in quantity
by the institutions under which he lives
and has an equal right
to express his judgment,
although the weight
of his judgment
may not be equal in amount
when it enters into the pooled result
to that of others.

In short,
each one is equally an individual
and entitled to equal opportunity
of development of his own capacities,
be they large or small in range.

Moreover,
each has needs of his own,
as significant to him
as those of others are to them.

The very fact
of natural and psychological inequality
is all the more reason
for establishment by law
of equality of opportunity,
since otherwise the former
becomes a means of oppression
of the less gifted.
John Dewey, 1937

On every side of us are men
who hunt perpetually
for their personal Northwest Passage,
too often sacrificing
health, strength, and life itself
to the search;
and who shall say
they are not happier
in their vain but hopeful quest
than wiser, duller folks
who sit at home,
venturing nothing
and, with sour laughs,
deriding the seekers
for that fabled thoroughfare?
Kenneth Roberts, 1937

It is after hours
and most of the people have gone home.
There is a chess game
in the office of the production manager
and a light still burns in the cashier's cage.
From the outer room
comes the untutored click of a typewriter—
an office boy is taking the Y.M.C.A. course in advertising.

Across the areaway
a man bends over his desk, writing.
A green visor shades his eyes.
From his twenty-eighth story window
as he glances up from time to time
he can look down on the jewelry of lights.
It is after hours,
but he works on.
He will whip his copy
into finished form before he leaves.

One of the layout men
has put his drawing board aside
and is going out to the elevators.
Under his arm he carries a tissue pad.
A new idea is stirring in his mind.
It will be roughed out in pencil before morning comes.
Six months from now
you will feel it
tugging at your purse strings.

It is after hours
and most of the people have gone home.

But out in Bronxville and Great Neck,
in London and Paris,
in Chicago and San Francisco—
in hotel rooms,
on Pullman cars,
on speeding planes
and ocean liners
this company's people
are thinking about other people's businesses,
working for men
who are all unaware such work is going on.
A few hurried notes
scrawled on the back of an old envelope tonight
may be the key to next year's
most productive advertising campaign.
Between the acts at the theatre
an idea may come that will make sales history.
At home beneath the reading lamp
a man may solve a merchandising problem.
Once a famous trademark
came back from a camping trip.

These are phases of our service
that perhaps not even our own clients
have ever thought of before.
There is no mention of it
in our Terms and Conditions.
But all our clients
have been the gainer for it
and will be many times again.
Why such devotion on the part of men
who have already given us their day?
Of no one here is asked more than he can do.
The client does not require it.

Again, why?
Anyone who deals regularly with men
will tell you this is the kind of work
that money alone cannot buy.
It is work done purely of free will
and its real pay is pride in work well done.
Those who understand the creative mind
will know just what we mean by that.
They know that the good workman,
in advertising as elsewhere, asks no question save,
how well can this be done?

This, too, was written after hours.
Erwin, Wasey & Company, Inc., 1939

The western land,
nervous under the beginning change.
The Western States,
nervous as horses before a thunderstorm.
The great owners,
nervous, sensing a change,
knowing nothing of the nature of the change.
The great owners,
striking at the immediate thing,
the widening government,
the growing labor unity;
striking at new taxes, at plans;
not knowing these things are results, not causes.
Results, not causes; results, not causes.
The causes lie deep and simply—
the causes are a hunger in the stomach,
multiplied a million times;
a hunger in a single soul,
hunger for joy and some security,
multiplied a million times;
muscles and mind aching to grow, to work, to create,
multiplied a million times.
The last clear definite function of man—
muscles aching to work,
minds aching to create beyond the single need—
this is man.
To build a wall, to build a house, a dam,
and in the wall and house and dam
to put something of Manself, and to Manself
take back something of the wall, the house, the dam;
to take hard muscles from the lifting,
to take the clear lines and form from conceiving.

For man,
unlike any other thing
organic or inorganic in the universe,
grows beyond his work,
walks up the stairs of his concepts,
emerges ahead of his accomplishments.
This you may say of man—
when theories change and crash,
when schools, philosophies,
when narrow dark alleys of thought,
national, religious, economic,
grow and disintegrate,
man reaches,
stumbles forward, painfully,
mistakenly sometimes.
Having stepped forward,
he may slip back,
but only half a step, never the full step back.
This you may say and know it and know it.
And this you can know—
fear the time when Manself
will not suffer and die for a concept,
for this one quality is the foundation of Manself,
and this one quality is man,
distinctive in the universe.
John Steinbeck, 1939

If we consider men and women generally,
and apart from their professions or occupations,
there is only one situation I can think of
in which they almost
pull themselves up by their bootstraps,
making an effort to read better
than they usually do.

When they are in love
and are reading a love letter,
they read it for all they are worth.
They read every word three ways;
they read between the lines
and in the margins;
they read the whole in terms of the parts,
and each part in terms of the whole;
they grow sensitive to context and ambiguity,
to insinuation and implication;
they perceive the color of words,
the odor of phrases,
and the weight of sentences.
They may even take the punctuation
into account.
Then, if never before or after, they read.
Mortimer Adler, 1940

It is men at work.
It is the storm-tossed fishermen
coming into Gloucester
and Providence
and Astoria.
It is the farmer riding his great machine
in the dust of harvest,
the dairyman going to the barn before sunrise,
the lineman mending the broken wire,
the miner drilling for the blast.
It is the servants of fire
in the murky splendor of Pittsburgh,
between the Allegheny and the Monongahela,
the trucks rumbling through the night,
the locomotive engineer
bringing the train in on time,
the pilot in the clouds,
the riveter running along the beam
a hundred feet in the air.
It is the clerk in the office,
the housewife doing the dishes
and sending the children off to school.
It is the teacher, doctor and parson
tending and helping, body and soul,
for small reward....

It is a great number of people on pilgrimage,
common and ordinary people,
charged with the usual human failings,
yet filled with such a hope
as never caught the imaginations and the hearts
of any nation on earth before.

The hope of liberty.
The hope of justice.
The hope of a land
in which a man can stand straight,
without fear,
without rancor.

The land and the people and the flag—
the land a continent,
the people of every race,
the flag a symbol
of what humanity may aspire to
when the wars are over and the barriers are down;
to these each generation
must be dedicated
and consecrated anew,
to defend with life itself, if need be,
but, above all,
in friendliness,
in hope,
in courage,
to live for.
R.L. *Duffus, 1940*

51 Throughout the centuries were men
who took first steps down the roads
armed with nothing but their own vision.
Their goals differed
but they all had this in common:
that the step was first,
the road new,
the vision unborrowed
and the response they received —
hatred.
The great creators —
the thinkers,
the artists,
the scientists,
the inventors —
stood alone against the men of their time.
Ayn Rand, 1943

The company commander said to me,
"Every man in this company deserves the Silver Star."

We walked around in the olive grove
where the men of the company
were sitting on the edges of their foxholes,
talking or cleaning their gear.

"Let's go over here," he said.
"I want to introduce you to my personal hero."

I figured
that the lieutenant's own "personal hero,"
out of a whole company of men
who deserved the Silver Star,
must be a real soldier indeed.

Then the company commander
introduced me to Sgt. Frank Eversole,
who shook hands sort of timidly and said,
"Pleased to meet you,"
and then didn't say any more.

I could tell by his eyes
and by his slow and courteous speech
when he did talk that he was a Westerner.
Conversation with him was sort of hard,
but I didn't mind his reticence
for I know how Westerners like to size people up first.

The sergeant wore a brown stocking cap
on the back of his head.

His eyes were the piercing kind.
I noticed his hands—
they were outdoor hands, strong and rough.

Later in the afternoon
I came past his foxhole again,
and we sat and talked a little while alone.
We didn't talk about the war,
but mainly about our West,
and just sat and made figures on the ground
with sticks as we talked.

We got started that way,
and in the days that followed
I came to know him well.
He is to me,
and to all those with whom he serves,
one of the great men of the war.

Frank Eversole's nickname is "Buck."
The other boys in the company
sometimes called him "Buck Overshoes,"
simply because Eversole sounds a bit like "overshoes."

Buck was a cowboy before the war.
He was born in the little town of Missouri Valley, Iowa,
and his mother still lives there.
But Buck went West on his own before he was sixteen,
and ever since has worked as a ranch hand.
He is twenty-eight, and unmarried.

He worked a long time around Twin Falls, Idaho,
and then later down in Nevada.
Like so many cowboys, he made the rodeos in season.

He was never a star or anything.
Usually he just rode the broncs
out of the chute for pay—seven-fifty a ride.
Once he did win a fine saddle.
He has ridden at Cheyenne and the other big rodeos.

Like any cowboy, he loves animals.
Here in Italy one afternoon
Buck and some other boys were pinned down
inside a one-room stone shed
by terrific German shellfire.
As they sat there,
a frightened mule came charging through the door.
There simply wasn't room inside
for men and mule both,
so Buck got up and shooed him out the door.
Thirty feet from the door a direct hit killed the mule.
Buck has always felt guilty about it.

Another time Buck ran onto a mule
that was down and crying in pain
from a bad shell wound.
Buck took his .45 and put a bullet through its head.
"I wouldn't have shot him
except he was hurtin' so," Buck says.

Buck Eversole has the Purple Heart
and two Silver Stars for bravery.
He is cold and deliberate in battle.
His commanders depend more on him
than on any other man.
He has been wounded once,
and had countless narrow escapes.
He has killed many Germans.

He is the kind of man you instinctively
feel safer with than with other people.
He is not helpless like most of us. He is practical.
He can improvise, patch things, fix things.

His grammar is the unschooled grammar
of the plains and the soil.
He uses profanity, but never violently.
Even in the familiarity of his own group
his voice is always low.
He is such a confirmed soldier by now
that he always says "sir" to any stranger.
It is impossible
to conceive of his doing anything dishonest.

After the war Buck will go back West
to the land he loves.
He wants to get a little place
and feed a few head of cattle, and be independent.

"I don't want to be just a ranch hand no more,"
  he says.
"It's all right and I like it all right,
  but it's a rough life and it don't get you nowhere.
  When you get a little older
  you kinda like a place of your own."

Buck Eversole has no hatred for Germans.
He kills because he's trying to keep alive himself.
The years roll over him
and the war becomes his only world,
and battle his only profession.
He armors himself with a philosophy
of acceptance of what may happen.

"I'm mighty sick of it all," he says very quietly,
"but there ain't no use to complain.
   I just figured it this way,
   that I've been given a job to do and I've got to do it.
   And if I don't live through it,
   there's nothing I can do about it."

In Italy, February 22, 1944 —
Buck Eversole is a platoon sergeant
in an infantry company.
 That means he has charge
 of about forty front-line fighting men.
He has been at the front for more than a year.
 War is old to him
 and he has become almost the master of it.
 He is a senior partner now in the institution of death.
 His platoon has turned over many times
 as battle whittles down the old ones
 and the replacement system brings up the new ones.
 Only a handful now are veterans.

"It gets so it kinda gets you, seein' these new kids,"
   Buck told me one night
   in his slow, barely audible Western voice,
   so full of honesty and sincerity.
"Some of them have just got fuzz on their faces,
   and don't know what it's all about,
   and they're scared to death.
   No matter what, some of them are bound to get killed."

 We talked about some of the other old-time noncoms
   who could take battle themselves,
   but had gradually grown morose under the responsibility
   of leading green boys to their slaughter.

Buck spoke of one sergeant especially,
a brave and hardened man,
who went to his captain and asked him
to be reduced to a private in the lines.

"I know it ain't my fault that they get killed,"
  Buck finally said.
"And I do the best I can for them,
  but I've got so I feel like it's me killin' 'em
  instead of a German.
  I've got so I feel like a murderer.
  I hate to look at them when the new ones come in."

Buck himself has been fortunate.
Once he was shot through the arm.
His own skill and wisdom have saved him many times.
But luck has saved him countless other times.

One night Buck and an officer
took refuge from shelling
in a two-room Italian stone house.
As they sat there,
a shell came through the wall of the far room,
crossed the room and buried itself in the middle wall
with its nose pointing upward.
It didn't go off.

Another time
Buck was leading his platoon on a night attack.
They were walking in Indian file.
Suddenly a mine went off,
and killed the entire squad following Buck.
He himself had miraculously walked
through the mine field without hitting a one.

One day Buck went stalking
a German officer in close combat,
and wound up with the German
on one side of a farmhouse and Buck on the other.
They kept throwing grenades over the house
at each other without success.
Finally Buck stepped around one corner of the house,
and came face to face with the German,
who'd had the same idea.

Buck was ready and pulled the trigger first.
His slug hit the German just above the heart.
The German had a wonderful pair of binoculars
slung over his shoulders,
and the bullet smashed them to bits.
Buck had wanted some German binoculars
for a long time.

The ties that grow up between men
who live savagely and die relentlessly together
are ties of great strength.
There is a sense of fidelity to each other
among little corps of men
who have endured so long
and whose hope in the end can be but so small.

One afternoon while I was with the company,
Sgt. Buck Eversole's turn came
to go back to rest camp for five days.
The company was due to attack that night.

Buck went to his company commander and said,
"Lieutenant, I don't think I better go.
I'll stay if you need me."

The lieutenant said,
"Of course I need you, Buck, I always need you.
But it's your turn and I want you to go.
In fact, you're ordered to go."

The truck taking the few boys
away to rest camp left just at dusk.
It was drizzling and the valleys
were swathed in a dismal mist.
Artillery of both sides
flashed and rumbled around the horizon.
The encroaching darkness was heavy and foreboding.

Buck came to the little group
of old-timers in the company
with whom I was standing, to say goodbye.
You'd have thought he was leaving forever.
He shook hands all around,
and his smile seemed sick and vulnerable.
He was a man stalling off his departure.

He said,
"Well, good luck to you all."
And then he said,
" I'll be back in just five days."
He said goodbye all around and slowly started away.
But he stopped and said goodbye all around again,
and he said,
"Well, good luck to you all."

I walked with him toward the truck in the dusk.
He kept his eyes on the ground,
and I think he would have cried if he knew how,
and he said to me very quietly:

"This is the first battle I've ever missed
   that this battalion has been in.
   Even when I was in the hospital with my arm
   they were in bivouac.
  This will be the first one I've ever missed.
   I sure do hope they have good luck."

   And then he said:
"I feel like a deserter."

   He climbed in,
   and the truck dissolved in the blackness.
   I went back and lay down
   on the ground
   among my other friends,
   waiting for the night orders to march.
   I lay there in the darkness thinking—
   terribly touched by the great simple devotion
   of this soldier who was a cowboy—
   and thinking of the millions far away at home
   who must remain forever
   unaware of the powerful fraternalism
   in the ghastly brotherhood of war.
   Ernie Pyle, 1944

Possessed of a mind utterly
impatient with time,
he labored unceasingly
to shove more than 60 minutes into an hour,
more than 24 hours into a day.
Impatience drove him
to try to accomplish in a day that
which took other men a week.
He was impatient that the solution
of a scientific problem
should elude him for even a week,
although he was known
to spend months and even years
before forcing some mystery of science
to yield to his groping intellect.

Yet, with all this driving impatience,
he never forgot how to be patient
with those with whom he lived and worked,
and with those he loved.
For this was his mark of true genius.
Mrs. Thomas Alva Edison, 1947

We are separated by the chasm
between the ox-cart and the jet engine,
between the grist mill and the cyclotron,
between a man wresting his own living
out of a wilderness farm
and the citizen whose livelihood
depends on the successful functioning
of an entire and complex national economy.

The impact on us
of every international fact and crisis
is immediate.
We are seldom free from anxiety
as each day's events
crowd instantly upon our attention.
Pressure groups often pretend to a moral purpose
that examination proves to be false.
The vote-seeker rarely hesitates to appeal to all
that is selfish in humankind.
Ruthless individuals,
whether they classify themselves as capitalists,
spokesmen of labor,
social reformers or politicians,
glibly promise us prosperity
for our support of their personal
but carefully concealed ambitions.
False teachers, who magnify acknowledged errors
in the practice of democracy,
attempt to destroy our faith
in man's right to self-government.
As we seek to conserve what is good and sound
even while we boldly explore and test new ways,

we are belabored by the demagogues of right and left;
both of whom would turn back the clock of history
to the days of regimented humanity.
In such a maelstrom of facts
and crises and false counsel,
the guideposts to individual duty and action
become obscured.

Infallible counsel for each of us
is to be found within our valid hopes
and aspirations and ideals as human beings,
so clearly understood by our colonial forebears.
The simple faith,
the unshakeable conviction
they held in man's individual rights
and his equality before the law and God,
is the most priceless jewel
in all the vast spiritual and material heritage
those men and women bequeathed to us.
We cannot afford
to lose their sharp sense of basic values....

Every American
is a free member of a mighty partnership
that has at its command all the pooled strength
of Western Civilization—
spiritual ideals, political experience,
social purpose, scientific wealth,
industrial prowess.
There is no limit,
other than our own resolve,
to the temporal goals we set before ourselves—
as free individuals joined in a team with our fellows;
as a free nation in the community of nations.

The modern preachers
of the paternalistic state permit themselves
to be intimidated by circumstances.
Blinding themselves
to the inevitable growth of despotism,
they—craven-like—seek,
through government,
assurance that they can forever
count upon a full stomach and warm cloak
or—perhaps—the sinister-minded among them think,
by playing upon our fears,
to become the masters of our lives.

In the years ahead
the fundamental struggle of our time
may be decided—between those
who would further apply to our daily lives
the concept of individual freedom and quality;
and those who would subordinate the individual
to the dictates of the state.
You will participate in the fight.
Dwight D. Eisenhower, 1949

I'm thinking of a program
for youngsters of senior high school age
and first and second year college.
My plan is to address assemblies
of high schools and colleges
on citizenship, political responsibility,
and the duty a citizen owes to the Republic
of which he is a citizen.

I want to give high schools
and small colleges preference.
I have an idea that 100 schools with 1,000 students
are of much more value to the country
than two schools with 50,000 students.

The objective is to build character,
find brain power and make responsible citizens
to keep the freedom of the individual intact.

Personal contact with instructors of character
is absolutely essential to these objectives.
Mass production of college graduates
is not the answer to an educated citizenship.

When the pioneers came
into the Ohio-Mississippi-Missouri valley
the first thing they thought of
after shelter and safety for their families
was education for the children.
In every settlement a church was built
and then a school house—
sometimes one building for both purposes.

Some of the greatest men
of the 19th century in our great nation
had to make the hardest kind
of struggle for education.
The fundamentals,
reading, writing and arithmetic,
were hard to obtain.

As the settlements grew
and communications improved
great schools
both religious and secular
grew also.
I am anxious to see
that thirst for knowledge
encouraged at the base.

The GI Bill of Rights proved conclusively
that young men from 18 to 26
after some experience thirst for learning
and that they are willing to work hard
and at some disadvantage for an education.

My definition of an education
is the lighting of that spark which is called
a "thirst for information or knowledge."
A college graduate
with the right sort of instruction
should find at his graduation
that he is only at the door of knowledge.
He should have learned
in going through his schooling
where to find the information on the subjects
that make for scholarship.

If he hasn't learned that,
the time spent in school
has been wasted for no good purpose.

If, when he comes out of school,
that thirst for learning has been brought out
he never ceases to find fields for study
that open up endlessly before him.

The old idea
that grammar, rhetoric, logic,
arithmetic, geometry, music and astronomy
constitute the basis of an education
is just as true now as it always has been.

Archimedes, Aristotle, Euclid, Galileo,
Leonardo da Vinci, Sir Isaac Newton, Einstein
all started from these fundamentals,
as did the great literary lights
and the great musicians.

So let's not forget
basic principles based on character.
Harry S. Truman

Our tragedy today
is a general and universal physical fear
so long sustained by now
that we can even bear it.
There are no longer problems of the spirit.
There is only the question:
When will I be blown up?
Because of this,
the young man or woman writing today
has forgotten the problems of the human heart
in conflict with itself
which alone can make good writing
because only that is worth writing about,
worth the agony and the sweat.

He must learn them again.
He must teach himself
that the basest of all things is to be afraid;
and, teaching himself that, forget it forever,
leaving no room in his workshop for anything
but the old verities and truths of the heart,
the old universal truths lacking
which any story is ephemeral and doomed—
love and honor and pity and pride
and compassion and sacrifice.
Until he does so, he labors under a curse.
He writes not of love but of lust,
or defeats in which nobody loses anything of value,
of victories without hope,
and, worst of all, without pity or compassion.
His griefs grieve on no universal bones, leaving no scars.
He writes not of the heart but of the glands.

Until he learns these things,
he will write as though
he stood among and watched the end of man.
I decline to accept the end of man.
It is easy enough to say
that man is immortal simply
because he will endure:
that when the last ding-dong of doom
has clanged and faded
from the last worthless rock
hanging tideless in the last red and dying evening,
that even then there will still be one more sound:
that of his puny inexhaustible voice, still talking.
I refuse to accept this.
I believe that man will not merely endure:
he will prevail.
He is immortal,
not because he alone among creatures
has an inexhaustible voice,
but because he has a soul,
a spirit capable of compassion
and sacrifice and endurance.
The poet's, the writer's duty
is to write about these things.
It is his privilege to help man endure
by lifting his heart, by reminding him
of the courage and honor and hope and pride
and compassion and pity and sacrifice
which have been the glory of his past.
The poet's voice
need not merely be the record of man,
it can be one of the props,
the pillars to help him endure and prevail.
William Faulkner, 1950

Now it is done.
Now the story ends.
And there is no way to tell it.
The art of fiction is dead.
Reality has strangled invention.
Only the utterly impossible,
the inexpressibly fantastic,
can ever be plausible again.

Down on the green and white
and earth-brown geometry of the playing field,
a drunk tries to break through the ranks
of ushers marshaled along the foul lines
to keep profane feet off the diamond.
The ushers thrust him back
and he lunges at them,
struggling in the clutch of two or three men.
He breaks free, and four or five tackle him.
He shakes them off,
bursts through the line,
runs head-on into a special park cop,
who brings him down with a flying tackle.

Here comes a whole platoon of ushers.
They lift the man and haul him,
twisting and kicking, back across the first-base line.
Again he shakes loose and crashes the line.
He is through.
He is away, weaving out toward center field,
where cheering thousands
are jammed beneath the windows
of the Giants' clubhouse.

At heart, our man is a Giant, too.
He never gave up.

From center field
comes burst upon burst of cheering.
Pennants are waving,
uplifted fists are brandished, hats are flying.
Again and again the dark clubhouse windows
blaze with the light of photographers' flash bulbs.
Here comes that same drunk out of the mob,
back across the green turf to the infield.
Coattails flying,
he runs the bases, slides into third.
Nobody bothers him now.

And the story remains to be told,
the story of how the Giants
won the 1951 pennant in the National League.
The tale of their barreling run
through August and September and into October....
Of the final day of the season,
when they won the championship
and started home with it from Boston,
to hear on the train
how the dead, defeated Dodgers
had risen from the ashes
in the Philadelphia twilight....
Of the three-game playoff
in which they won,
and lost,
and were losing again
with one out in the ninth inning
yesterday when—
Oh, why bother?

Maybe this is the way to tell it:
Bobby Thomson,
a young Scot from Staten Island,
delivered a timely hit yesterday
in the ninth inning
of an enjoyable game of baseball
before 34,320 witnesses in the Polo Grounds....
Or perhaps this is better:

"Well!" said Whitey Lockman,
standing on second base in the second inning
of yesterday's playoff game
between the Giants and Dodgers.

"Ah, there," said Bobby Thomson,
pulling into the same station
after hitting a ball to left field.
"How've you been?"

"Fancy," Lockman said, "meeting you here!"

"Oops!" Thomson said. "Sorry."

And the Giants' first chance
for a big inning against Don Newcombe
disappeared as they tagged Thomson out.
Up in the press section,
the voice of Willie Goodrich
came over the amplifiers
announcing a macabre statistic:
"Thomson has now hit safely in fifteen consecutive games."
Just then the floodlights were turned on,
enabling the Giants
to see and count their runners on each base.

It wasn't funny, though,
because it seemed for so long
that the Giants weren't going to get another chance
like the one Thomson squandered
by trying to take second base
with a playmate already there.
They couldn't hit Newcombe,
and the Dodgers couldn't do anything wrong.

Sal Maglie's most splendorous pitching
would avail nothing
unless New York could match the run Brooklyn
had scored in the first inning.

The story was winding up,
and it wasn't the happy ending
that such a tale demands.
Poetic justice was a phrase without meaning.

Now it was the seventh inning
and Thomson was up,
with runners on first and third base, none out.
Pitching a shutout in Philadelphia last Saturday night,
pitching again in Philadelphia on Sunday,
holding the Giants scoreless this far,
Newcombe had now gone twenty-one innings
without allowing a run.

He threw four strikes to Thomson.
Two were fouled off out of play.
Then he threw a fifth.
Thomson's fly scored Monte Irvin.
The score was tied.
It was a new ball game.

Wait a moment, though.
Here's Pee Wee Reese
hitting safely in the eighth.
Here's Duke Snider
singling Reese to third.
Here's Maglie
wild-pitching a run home.
Here's Andy Pafko
slashing a hit through Thomson for another score.
Here's Billy Cox
batting still another home.
Where does his hit go?
Where else?
Through Thomson at third.

So it was the Dodgers' ball game, 4 to 1,
and the Dodgers' pennant.
So all right.
Better get started and beat the crowd home.
That stuff in the ninth inning?
That didn't mean anything.

A single by Al Dark.
A single by Don Mueller.
Irvin's pop-up,
Lockman's one-run double.
Now the corniest possible sort
of Hollywood schmaltz—
stretcher-bearers plodding away
with an injured Mueller between them,
symbolic of the Giants themselves.

There went Newcombe
and here came Ralph Branca.

Who's at bat?
Thomson again?
He beat Branca
with a home run the other day.
Would Charley Dressen order him walked,
putting the winning run on base,
to pitch to the dead-end kids
at the bottom of the batting order?
No, Branca's first pitch was called a strike.

The second pitch—
well, when Thomson reached first base
he turned and looked toward the left-field stands.
Then he started jumping straight up in the air,
again and again.
Then he trotted around the bases,
taking his time.
Ralph Branca turned and started for the clubhouse.
The number on his uniform looked huge.
Thirteen.
Red Smith, 1951

[Following his baseball career,
Bobby Thomson joined Westvaco,
completing a distinguished career in sales in 1986.]

58 They say you can't do it,
    but sometimes that isn't always true.
    Casey Stengel

Expecting the best
means that you put your whole heart
(i.e., the central essence of your personality)
into what you want to accomplish.
People are defeated in life
not because of lack of ability,
but for lack of wholeheartedness.
They do not wholeheartedly expect to succeed.
Their heart isn't in it,
which is to say
they themselves are not fully given.
Results do not yield themselves to the person
who refuses to give himself to the desired results.

A major key to success in this life,
to attaining that which you deeply desire,
is to be completely released
and throw all there is of yourself
into your job or any project
in which you are engaged.
In other words,
whatever you are doing,
give it all you've got.
Give every bit of yourself.
Hold nothing back.
Life cannot deny itself to the person
who gives life his all.
But most people, unfortunately, don't do that.
In fact, very few people do,
and this is a tragic cause of failure,
or, if not failure,
it is the reason we only half attain....

In this process of achieving the best
it is important
to know where you want to go in life.
You can reach your goal,
your best dreams can come true,
you can get where you want to go
only if you know what your goal is.
Your expectation must have a clearly defined objective.
Lots of people get nowhere
simply because they do not know
where they want to go.
They have no clear-cut, precisely defined purpose.
You cannot expect the best if you think aimlessly. . . .

A man
who is self-reliant, positive, optimistic,
and undertakes his work
with the assurance of success
magnetizes his condition.
He draws to himself
the creative powers of the universe.
Norman Vincent Peale, 1952

60   There is in most Americans
       some spark of idealism,
       which can be fanned into a flame.
       It takes sometimes a divining rod
       to find what it is;
       but when found,
       and that means often,
       when disclosed to the owners,
       the results are often extraordinary.
       Louis D. Brandeis

I lean back in the wicker seat,
running my eyes
once more over the instruments.
Nothing wrong there.
They all tell the proper story.
Even the tachometer needle is in place,
with the engine idling....
I turn again to the problem of take-off.
It will be slow at best.
Can the engine stand
such a long ground run
at wide-open throttle,
or will it overheat and start to miss?

Suppose I *can* hold the runway,
suppose I *do* get off the ground—
will fog close in and force me back?
Suppose the ceiling drops to zero—
I can't fly blind
with this overload of fuel; but the wheels
have doubtful safety factors for a landing.
Shall I cut the switch and wait another day
for confirmation of good weather?
But if I leave now,
I'll have a head start
on both the Fokker and the Bellanca.
Once in the air,
I can nurse my engine all the way to Paris—
there'll be no need to push it in a race.
And the moon's past full—
it will be three weeks to the next one;
conditions then may be still worse.

Wind, weather, power, load—
gradually these elements stop churning in my mind.
It's less a decision of logic than of feeling,
the kind of feeling that comes
when you gauge the distance to be jumped
between two stones across a brook.
Something within you
disengages itself from your body
and travels ahead with your vision
to make the test.
You can feel it try the jump as you stand looking.
Then uncertainty gives way to the conviction
that it *can* or can't be done.
Sitting in the cockpit,
in seconds, minutes long,
the conviction surges through me
that the wheels *will* leave the ground,
that the wings *will* rise above the wires,
that it *is* time to start the flight.

I buckle my safety belt,
pull goggles down over my eyes,
turn to the men at the blocks, and nod.
Frozen figures leap to action.
A yank on the ropes—the wheels are free....
Charles A. Lindbergh, 1953

62 There is no substitute for excellence,
    not even success.
    I.F. Stone

63 To be nobody-but-yourself—
    in a world
    which is doing its best,
    night and day,
    to make you everybody else—
    means to fight the hardest battle
    which any human being can fight;
    and never stop fighting.
    E.E. Cummings

"Hell, I hire anybody,"
Harold Ross told Ralph Ingersoll
in the summer of 1925
when Ingersoll called
on the editor of the *New Yorker*,
asked for a job, and got one.
It wasn't as simple as it sounds, though.
Ingersoll had appeared in the editor's office
dressed in a Palm Beach suit
he had bought for the occasion,
and Ross had talked to him
for only a few minutes,
gesticulating widely,
when his big right hand struck an inkwell.
Suddenly Ingersoll's new suit was dripping with ink
and Ross was covered with embarrassment.
Ingersoll had almost reached the office door
on what he was sure
was his way out of Ross's life
when the editor shouted,
"You're hired!"
And then, a few moments later, sighed,
"Hell, I hire anybody."

From then on
Ross hired anybody, and everybody,
in his frantic and ceaseless search
for the Fountain of Perfection.
A few of us came to realize
that he didn't really want to find it
whether he knew it or not;
that the quest itself was what kept him going.

If he had found the Redeemer
who, in Cabell's words, would make everything
as "neat as a trivet or an apple-pie," he would have
grasped his own starry scheme of things entire,
smashed it all to bits, and then
remodeled it nearer to his heart's desire,
or his mind's illusion, or whatever it was.
A team of Freuds would have
a hard time putting a finger
on the Imp of the Perverse in Ross's psyche.
I think he was looking
for two separate kinds of Miracle Men:
the administrative genius
who would sit at a Central Desk, push buttons,
and produce Instant Perfection of organization,
and a literary wizard
who would wave a magic wand over writers and artists
and conjure up Instant Perfection in prose,
drawings, and all other contents of the magazine.

H.W. Ross, being neither artist nor poet,
was not equipped to bring "grace and measure"
out of the chaos of man on earth,
for his heart's ease or his peace of mind,
but there was in him something of the powerful urge
that has animated the human male
from Sir Percival to Pasteur,
from Marco Polo to Admiral Peary.
He never knew exactly what he was after,
since he didn't have much self-knowledge
and was afraid of introspection, but I think
he hoped it would be as shining as the Holy Grail,
or as important as the Northwest Passage
or as rewarding as the pot of gold.

He was afraid, though, that a Gorgon
would pop up at any time to frustrate him,
or a Questyng Beast, or a Gordian knot,
and he realized that he damn well better
have a Perseus on hand to help him,
or a Palamedes, or an Alexander the Great.
These romantic comparisons would, I am sure,
move psychiatrists to ridicule; they would find
in Sir Harold not a romantic, but a mixed-up
modern man driven by the well-known compulsion
to build with one hand and tear down with the other.
Well, that urge was in him, too,
along with fixation, defense mechanism,
inferiority complex, and all the rest.

Many of us who went with him on his Quest,
part of or all the way,
often became bored or infuriated,
and wanted to quit,
and there were scores who did quit
and found an easier way to live and make a living.
A few of us could not quit.
We had put on the armor
and strapped on the sword
and we were stuck with them.
Once, when E.B. White had taken all he could,
or thought he had,
he said he was quitting and went home.
Ross paced his office all afternoon
and then got White on the phone in his apartment.
"You *can't* quit," he roared.
"This isn't a magazine—it's a Movement!"
Andy did not leave the Movement.
James Thurber, 1957

I owe most of everything
to football...
a game which demands from each man
a contribution of spirit!
This spirit
is the cohesive force
that really binds
eleven hardened, talented men
into winners.
The many (physical) hurts
seem a small price to pay
for having won,
and there's no reason at all
that is adequate for having lost!

To the winner
there is 100 percent elation,
100 percent laughter, 100 percent fun...
and to the loser
the only thing left
is 100 percent resolution,
and 100 percent determination.

Football is a game,
I think,
a great deal like life,
in that a man's personal commitment
be toward success...
to victory...
ultimate victory,
which must be pursued
with all of one's might!

Each week
there is a new encounter...
each year
a new challenge...
the color and display
linger only in memory.
But the spirit...
the will to win...
and the will to excel—
these are the things that endure!
These are the qualities
which are so much more important
than any of the events which occasion them!

The quality of any man's life
has *got* to be a full measure of that man's
personal commitment to excellence...
and to victory
regardless what field he may be in!

I would say that this is my football creed.
Vince Lombardi, 1958

Leadership is particularly important
in the United States
because, unlike Europe and Asia,
no caste system has ever taken deep root in this country.
In the older, more static civilizations,
because of a long tradition
of monarchical and aristocratic rule,
the leader is, so to speak,
often "naturally" provided.
A distinguished family name, a title, a uniform—
sometimes all three combined—
may suffice to establish the authority and prestige.
His leadership position is rarely questioned;
his right to wield power or exert influence
is hardly challenged.
He is, in the well-known phrase, "to the manner born."

Not so in the United States.
Here, the leader first
has to prove himself to achieve his position,
and secondly, he has to exert himself to retain it.
This, in essence, is a part
of America's democratic dynamism.
It was recognized long ago
by an early democrat, Thomas Jefferson, that democracy,
by rejecting the idea and the practice of a caste system,
must therefore rely on what he called
a "natural aristocracy."
Nature, he said, scatters human talents
among all types of people, rich and poor alike,
and this reservoir of abilities must be used
for leadership and enrichment of democracy.

American life today
exemplifies Jefferson's conception
of a natural aristocracy.
Whether in business or government or the professions,
America's leaders are generally those
whose positions were attained
through individual effort and skill,
rather than birth.
Cases of inherited wealth and social status
do exist among the leaders,
but the majority,
including the last two Presidents of the United States,
come from modest homes.
Surveys indicate that most leaders—
mayors, presidents of civic organizations,
members of Congress, heads of industries—
are college graduates and, on community levels,
more than half of them have professional degrees.
The educational ladder—that is,
training for positions of power and influence—
still remains the primary avenue
of advancement in American life.
Think Magazine, IBM Corporation, 1959

The moment General Marshall entered a room,
everyone in it felt his presence.
It was a striking and communicated force.
His figure conveyed intensity,
which his voice, low, staccato, and incisive, reinforced.
It compelled respect.
It spread a sense of authority and of calm.
There was no military glamour about him
and nothing of the martinet.
Yet to all of us he was always
"General Marshall."
The title fitted him
as though he had been baptized with it.
He always identified himself over the telephone
as "General Marshall speaking."
It seemed wholly right, too.
I should never have dreamed
of addressing him as "Mr. Secretary";
and I have never heard anyone
but Mrs. Marshall call him "George."
The General expected to be treated with respect
and to treat others the same way.
This was the basis of his relationships.

President Truman has put his finger on
another foundation of General Marshall's character.
Never, wrote the President,
did General Marshall think about *himself*.
This is true and deeply significant.
The ego is the ultimate corrupter of man.
One who controls it has the strength of ten,
for then, truly, his heart is pure.

General Marshall's ego
never got between him and his task.
Justice Holmes said,
"If you want to hit a bird on the wing,
you must have all your will in a focus.
You must not be thinking about yourself, and, equally,
you must not be thinking about your neighbor;
you must be living in your eye on that bird.
Every achievement is a bird on the wing."
General Marshall lived in his eye on the task in hand.

With General Marshall self-control came,
as I suppose it always comes,
from self-discipline.
He was, in a phrase that has quite gone out of use,
in command of himself.
Dean Acheson, 1959

Part of being a leader is being able
to withstand the arrows of price competition.
A leader need not be the biggest
or the oldest company in its field,
but it's the one that stands out
because it is recognized as the best.
It wins price wars because its reputation
for excellence in its field
will not be obliterated by price-cutting.

A leader is also usually a living—
and very healthy—testimonial to the effectiveness
of an important marketing principle:
That in the long run
it profits you far more
to sell your product on its *value*
rather than on its *price*.

Almost everyone will agree
with that principle in theory;
but many violate it in practice.
It is often so easy to pick up quick sales
by promoting special prices or deals.
And it is so hard to resist the temptation
to fight fire with fire
when price-cutting competitors
are apparently hurting you.

Perhaps the main reason more manufacturers
do not sell on value rather than on price
is that selling on value
is far more difficult than selling on price.

It requires, of course, a product that *has* value.
But that is only the beginning.

It also requires
the marketing wisdom
to know what specific *character*
you should create for your product
to separate it most favorably
from all others of its kind.
 Then it requires the creative skill
to crystallize that character
on paper
or on the air waves,
and project it into the minds of the right people
at the right time...

It requires something else, too—
the lonely courage to stand out from the crowd,
to tell your own story consistently,
year in and year out,
regardless of the opportunistic tactics of competition.
Perhaps this is the rarest quality of all.
It is sometimes called Leadership.
William A. Marsteller, 1960

There are many varieties of excellence....
In the intellectual field alone
there are many kinds of excellence.
There is the kind of intellectual activity
that leads to a new theory,
and the kind that leads to a new machine.

And there is excellence in art,
in music, in craftsmanship,
in human relations, in technical work,
in leadership, in parental responsibilities.

Some kinds of excellence can be fostered
by the educational system,
and others must be fostered
outside the educational system.
Some kinds, managerial—may lead to worldly success,
and others, compassion—may not.

There are types of excellence
that involve doing something well
and types that involve
being a certain kind of person....

Anyone who looks at the way in which
the world judges his own contemporaries
will recognize the varied standards of judgment
which come into play.
But though in daily life
we recognize a good many kinds of high performance,
we rarely make this variety
explicit in our thinking about excellence....

Taking the whole span of history and literature,
the images of excellence are amply varied:
Confucius teaching the feudal lords
to govern wisely.
Leonidas defending the pass at Thermopylae.
Saint Francis preaching to the birds at Alviano.
Lincoln writing the second inaugural
"with malice toward none."
Mozart composing his first oratorio
at the age of eleven.
Galileo dropping weights from the Tower of Pisa.
Emily Dickinson jotting her "letters to the world"
on scraps of paper.
Florence Nightingale
nursing the wounded at Balaclava.
Eli Whitney pioneering the manufacture
of interchangeable parts....

Our society
cannot achieve greatness
unless individuals at many levels of ability
accept the need for high standards of performance
and strive to achieve those standards
within the limits possible for them...
We must foster a conception of excellence
which may be applied to every degree of ability
and to every socially acceptable activity...
We need excellent physicists
and excellent mechanics.
We need excellent cabinet members
and excellent first-grade teachers.
The tone and fiber of our society
depend upon a pervasive and almost universal
striving for good performance.

And we are not going to get
that kind of striving,
that kind of alert and proud attention to performance,
unless we can instruct the whole society
in a conception of excellence
that leaves room for everybody
who is willing to strive—
a conception of excellence which means
that whoever I am or whatever I am doing,
provided that I am engaged
in a socially acceptable activity,
some kind of excellence is within my reach....

We cannot have islands of excellence
in a sea of slovenly indifference to standards...

I am not saying that we can expect
every man to be excellent.
It would please me if this were possible:
I am not one of those
who believe that a goal is somehow unworthy
if everyone can achieve it.
But those who achieve excellence will be few at best.
All too many lack the qualities of mind or spirit
which would allow them
to conceive excellence as a goal,
or to achieve it if they conceived it.

But many more can achieve it than now do.
Many, many more can *try*
to achieve it than now do.
And the society is bettered
not only by those who achieve it
but by those who are trying....

Standards!
That is a word for every American
to write on his bulletin board....

The importance of competence
as a condition of freedom
has been widely ignored.
Keeping a free society free—
and vital and strong—
is no job for the half-educated and the slovenly.
Free men must be competent men....

But excellence implies more than competence.
It implies a striving for the highest standards
in every phase of life.
We need individual excellence in all its forms—
in every kind of creative endeavor,
in political life, in education, in industry—
in short, universally.

Those who are most deeply devoted
to a democratic society must be precisely the ones
who insist upon excellence,
who insist that free men are capable
of the highest standards of performance,
who insist that a free society can be a great society
in the richest sense of that phrase....

Free men must set their own goals...
If they have the wisdom and courage
to demand much of themselves—
as individuals and as a society—
they may look forward to long-continued vitality.
John W. Gardner, 1961

Managing an advertising agency
is like managing any other creative organization—
a research laboratory, a magazine,
an architect's office, a great kitchen.

Thirty years ago
I was a chef at the Hotel Majestic in Paris.
Henri Soulé of the Pavillon tells me
that it was probably the best kitchen there has ever been.

There were thirty-seven chefs in our brigade.
We worked like dervishes, sixty-three hours a week—
there was no trade union.
From morning to night
we sweated and shouted and cursed and cooked.
Every man jack was inspired by one ambition:
to cook better than any chef had ever cooked before.
Our *esprit de corps*
would have done credit to the Marines.

I have always believed
that if I could understand
how Monsieur Pitard, the head chef,
inspired such white-hot morale,
I could apply the same kind of leadership
to the management of my advertising agency.

To begin with,
he was the best cook in the whole brigade,
and we knew it.
He had to spend most of his time at his desk,
planning menus, scrutinizing bills, and ordering supplies,

but once a week
he would emerge from his glass-walled office
in the middle of the kitchen
and actually *cook* something.
A crowd of us always gathered around to watch,
spellbound by his virtuosity.
It was inspiring
to work for a supreme master.

(Following Chef Pitard's example,
 I still write occasional advertisements myself,
 to remind my brigade of copywriters
 that my hand has not lost its cunning.)

M. Pitard ruled with a rod of iron,
 and we were terrified of him.
There he sat in his glass cage, the *gros bonnet*,
 the arch symbol of authority.
Whenever I made a mistake in my work,
 I would look up to see
 if his gimlet eye had noticed it....

M. Pitard praised very seldom,
 but when he did, we were exalted to the skies.
When the President of France
 came to a banquet at the Majestic,
 the atmosphere in our kitchen was electric.
On one of these memorable occasions,
 I was covering frogs' legs with a white *chaud-froid* sauce,
 decorating each little thigh with an ornate leaf of chervil.
Suddenly I became aware that M. Pitard
 was standing beside me, watching.
I was so frightened
 that my knees knocked together and my hands trembled.

He took the pencil from his starched toque
and waved it in the air,
his signal for the whole brigade to gather.
Then he pointed at my frogs' legs
and said, very slowly and very quietly,
"That's how to do it."
I was his slave for life.

(Today I praise my staff
as rarely as Pitard praised his chefs,
in the hope that they too will appreciate it more
than a steady gush of appreciation.)....

M. Pitard taught me
exorbitant standards of service.
For example,
he once heard me tell a waiter
that we were fresh out of the *plat du jour*—
and almost fired me for it.
In a great kitchen, he said,
one must always honor
what one has promised on the menu.

(Today I see red when anybody
at Ogilvy, Benson *&* Mather tells a client
that we cannot produce an advertisement
or a television commercial
on the day we have promised it.
In the best establishments,
promises are always kept,
whatever it may cost in agony and overtime.)....

M. Pitard was a martinet
in making us keep the kitchen clean.

Twice a day
I had to scrape the wooden surface
of the larder table with a sharp plane.
Twice a day
the floor was scrubbed,
and clean sawdust put down.
Once a week
a bugcatcher scoured the kitchen
in search of roaches.
We were issued clean uniforms every morning.

(Today I am a martinet
in making my staff keep their offices shipshape.
A messy office creates an atmosphere of sloppiness,
and leads to the disappearance of secret papers.)....

During the service of luncheon and dinner,
M. Pitard stationed himself at the counter
where we cooks handed our dishes to the waiters.
He inspected every single dish
before it left the kitchen.
Sometimes he sent it back to the cook
for more work.
Always he reminded us
not to put too much on the plate—
"*pas trop!*"
He wanted the Majestic to make a profit.

(Today I inspect every campaign
before it goes to the client,
and send back many of them for more work.
And I share M. Pitard's passion for profit.)
David Ogilvy, 1963

Less than 10 percent of all salesmen
do more than 80 percent of all business.
They are the great salesmen,
and they make the great companies.

So let's all hire some!

Unfortunately, it's not that easy.

Great salesmen don't grow on trees.
Even if they did, we might have to wait a long time.
It takes 40 years to mature an oak,
at least half that long
to grow a great salesman.
That is, if you plant well in the first place.

The difference between
growing the tallest tree in the forest
and one of a hundred smaller saplings
is where the roots go.
The roots of a great salesman go deep,
far beyond knowing products,
or how to answer objections,
or how to open doors.

A good friend of ours,
who also happens to be a great salesman,
suggests that maybe it's time
we gave our young people the simple encouragement
to learn how to work in a society
where it is not always fashionable to work.
His advice is quite simple.

"First, find a young man, about 11½.
  Your son, or grandson,
   or the boy next door,
   or the one across the tracks will do.

"Next, clear up any misconceptions
  he might have
   about expecting something for nothing.
  Make sure he knows
  how to shake hands, and smile
  and say 'yes sir' and 'no sir,'
  and 'thank you' and 'how can I help.'

"Then give him encouragement
  and a chance to sell a product.
  He might try Cloverine Salve
  or *Grit* Magazine
  or the *National Observer*
  or one of a hundred other good products
  where he can earn a nickel or more
  each time he makes a sale.

"You might suggest a sidewalk to shovel,
  or a lawn to rake
  or some other service to sell
  where he won't get paid
  until the job is well done.

"Teach him how to do the job
  better than the next fellow.
  How to put the paper inside the door
  instead of out in the rain.
  How to trim around every tree
  when he mows the lawn.

"Remind him why promises are kept,
about being on time,
and how to use his talents
in helping others use theirs.
Let him taste the excitement
of earning a profit for honest work.
Let him enjoy the spirit of competition,
the disappointment of losing a customer
when someone else does the job better.
And let him find the will
to go back for a second chance."

Why do these things?

Well, some people are lucky enough
to be born with the will to work
and the motivation to excel.
Others have to be shown the way,
and if we do the showing, who knows?
Maybe someday, somewhere,
when your young man is ready to face the world,
someone will ask him
if he would like to be a salesman.

He won't ask:
"What's a salesman?"
Chances are, he's already one.
Maybe he'll even grow up to be a great one.

He's probably well on his way.

And what's wrong with that?
John C. Callihan, 1966

72 There is only one way to work— like hell.
    Bette Davis

When I was a boy in Commerce, Oklahoma,
the very best place to play ball,
except for the ball field
where the Commerce Merchants played,
was the "Alkali"—a flat stretch of plain
where lead-mine shafts had been sunk and abandoned,
and where chat-piles, heaps of exhausted ore,
some higher than houses,
made mile-long shadows in the early morning.
The dry summer winds would sift the alkali dust
from the tops of the chat-piles
and sprinkle it over the plains all around,
burning them bare of grass and undergrowth
until the whole area was hard-packed and barren
as a parade ground.
The cave-ins and the old shafts, closed off
by beaten fences any boy could climb over or through,
created a constant hazard,
yet it was not one that bore heavily on us.
The bad feature of the place, to a boy playing ball,
was the outfield, which went on and on,
without a ditch, or a brook,
or a fence, or an embankment,
just flat plain that stretched unbroken
to the back yards of Commerce.
A ball hit over an outfielder's head
meant a weary chase, for the hard ground
would hardly slow the ball at all,
and sometimes it would skip away
faster than a boy could run,
until it seemed bound to get back
to his own back yard before he did.

I think that endless outfield is the chief reason
why I became an infielder,
despite my lack of aptitude for that job.
When I got big enough
to have some say where I played,
I refused to play outfield on the Alkali.
When I was real small,
but still able to play ball with my betters,
I was not supposed to be out on the Alkali at all,
and if my mother caught me there,
as she did once or twice, she would haul me home
and really warm my britches.
People still told about children
who had fallen into the cave-ins and been killed,
but I had never known of any.
Still, my mother was bound that none
of her own young would tumble to an untimely death
down one of those black holes.
She did not object to my playing ball, however.
On the contrary, she and my father agreed
that there was nothing a growing boy
could do better than play baseball
as long as daylight would let him.
There were days when I left home
with nothing more than a Thermos jug of water,
to play ball from breakfast until dark,
without even a break for food,
and my parents sent me off with their blessing.

Baseball had long been my father's passion.
He named me—his oldest—
after a baseball hero of his own, Mickey Cochrane,
and my name was always Mickey,
not Michael, just Mickey.

All his youth my father had wanted me
to be a professional baseball player,
and like my grandfather, Charles Mantle,
he had played amateur and semi-pro ball
throughout our corner of the state.
While his aim had always been to play shortstop,
he was best at pitching
and when he did not pitch,
he played the outfield.
He never wanted to sit on the bench.
So it happened that my father,
who was known everywhere as Mutt Mantle,
although his name was Elven,
decided that if he couldn't
become a professional baseball player, I should.
He was almost comic in his determination
to make a baseball player out of his little boy.
When I was still in the cradle,
I had a knitted baseball cap;
and a pair of his old baseball pants were whittled down
to fit me before I was in kindergarten.
I believe too that he put a baseball
and a glove in my crib when I was still too new
to do much more than chew at them.
It was a wonder, I suppose,
that I did not turn against baseball,
from having it forced on me so young.
But instead I loved the game
with a fierce devotion that has never slackened.
Once I had learned to hit a ball with a bat,
I needed none of my father's urging to play the game.
Knowing that it pleased my father
to see me do well at the game
only made it twice as much fun to me....

He never drove me to play baseball,
for no one ever had to do that.
But he worked hard to help me improve
and he gave me good advice to follow
and played with me when he had the chance.
It wasn't the thought
of riches or fame that drove me.
I didn't think about those things.
I had no desire to leave home
or to get very far from Commerce
and the towns around us.
What did keep me driving hard,
from the time that I was ten,
to hit the ball better and farther
was first of all my own love for the game
and then my love for my father.
I knew from the time I was small
that every small victory I won,
and every solid hit I made
or prize I was awarded,
brought real joy to my father's heart.
Not long ago, when I read in the paper
that George Scott of the Boston Red Sox
had telephoned his mother to tell her
of being chosen for the All Star team,
I felt a tingle of sympathy.
And when I got on first base
against the Red Sox that day
and had a chance to talk to George,
I mentioned this to him and we agreed
that having someone
to share an accomplishment with,
someone you knew would get a thrill from it,
made the accomplishment twice as sweet....

Like all good fathers, he had let me beat him
in friendly matches when I was tiny,
but once I had grown man-size,
he treated me like a man,
and made no allowances.
I was fourteen when we raced that day
and he was thirty-three.

It may have been that year, or the year after,
that I received the Christmas present
I will remember all my life.
Christmas was always a thrilling day in our house,
as in most homes thereabouts,
for even though money was scarce,
my father saw to it that Santa Claus forgot no one
and he tried hard always to surprise us
with things we longed for.
The family was up early on Christmas morning,
usually before it was full day,
to see what lay under the tree.
This morning my present took my breath away.
It was a full-size professional model baseball glove,
carrying Marty Marion's autograph,
the best glove money could buy.
I knew exactly what it cost,
for I had yearned after it for a long time—it was $22,
about one-third of my father's weekly salary—
and I knew, as all poor boys do,
exactly what that amount of money
meant in a family like ours.
Of course, I doted on the glove
with an unholy passion, loving even the smell of it,
and I caressed and cared for it through the winter
as if it had been a holy relic.

But most of all,
my heart was bursting
with the realization of what a sacrifice like this
said about my father's love for me
and about his pride in my ability....

One day we had nothing for a bat
but a metal bedpost
and I, playing catcher,
and leaping too suddenly out to grab a pitch
and throw out a man stealing,
took the bedpost right in the back of the skull.
I was laid cold for an instant—
my first serious baseball injury—
but I was up and back in the game
before the pitcher had even cooled off....

Looking back on it now,
I don't believe I was even the best batter in town
when I was a schoolboy.
I had some playmates
who seemed to me much better ballplayers—
Bill Moseley for instance,
who became the head coach at Topeka.
Bill, incidentally, was the football player
I liked to pattern myself after.
Or at least he showed me
a style of play that appealed to me,
for he played like a madman,
going all out at every chance,
never giving up
until he was gang-tackled and immobile,
giving the game his full mind and full heart
all the time he was on the field.

I tried to do the same, and discovered
it actually multiplied the fun of the game
to immerse yourself in it this way.

But to get back to baseball:
I actually considered myself the worst player
of the lot I played with as a kid
because my fielding was always erratic.
But as I said before,
I was the one who had the father
to coach, encourage, and keep me playing.

By the time I was in my mid-teens,
baseball was so much a part of my life
that I had a hard time
believing there was anything much else.
When I wasn't playing baseball myself—
and I played some form of ball
every waking hour
when rain or snow or cold did not prevent it—
I was reading about baseball or watching it,
or shagging stray baseballs at the local field....

My father,
by that time, was doing his best
to get me a big league trial.
He had even carted me to St. Louis
to try to get me a tryout with the Browns,
but they were not interested
in kid shortstops at all.
The first major league scout to approach me,
as it turned out,
was a fellow well known in the area,
Runt Marr, who scouted for the Cardinals.

He came to my house one day
and asked me simply not to sign
with any other club
until he had a chance to make me an offer.
This put a chill of excitement
into my bones
but when days went by
with no further word from him,
I concluded there was not going to be
any offer at all from that quarter.

My fielding, I knew, was often sorry.
I had learned to charge a ground ball well,
and if I could get an angle on a ball,
I could field it cleanly
and get off a fast throw.
My arm was unusually strong
and my throws would really hum
across the diamond.
But when a ball came straight at me,
I was often undone.
Somehow it was almost impossible
for me to judge the speed
or the bounce of a ground ball like that.
I might back off foolishly,
letting the ball play me,
and then lose it altogether.
Or I would turn my head as it reached me
and the ball would skip by
or bounce right into my face.
I carried around uncounted fat lips in that day
from stopping ground balls with my mouth.
And the more often I got hit,
the more I would shy at such a ball.

Even the balls I fielded cleanly
did not always mean an out,
for I had a habit of rejoicing so
in the strength of my arm
that I would not take the time
to get a sure eye on the target.
I would just let fly with my full strength,
and often the ball
would sail untouched into the stands.

But my hitting just seemed to get better,
and my speed on drag bunts made it possible for me
to pull myself out of a batting slump
by legging out a few base-hits
almost any time I needed them.
I doted on fast balls.
Curves did not bother me but it was just
that I could get better distance on a fast ball,
and when I was ahead of the pitcher
and knew he would have to come in with a fast ball,
I could really bust it into small pieces.
This was what my local reputation was based on,
and when scouts came to see me,
they came to see me hit.

I had had my preview for Tom Greenwade
and nothing happened.
Then, on a sultry evening in 1949,
Tom drove with my father to another Whiz Kid game.
Rain cut the game short
and I dashed through the downpour
to Tom Greenwade's car,
to find my father sitting there
with Greenwade beside him.

I climbed into the back seat
and listened to the negotiations.
I'm not going to say my heart was in my mouth,
because I already knew Tom Greenwade
had seen me at my best.
But I was somewhat atremble inside
all the same
as I sat there in silence while the two men talked.

This was no
"We'll call you later" deal.
Greenwade was there to sign me to a contract.
Once I understood that, I don't believe
I'd have been distracted by a tornado,
much less by the pelting of rain on the car roof.
Greenwade was solemnly
outlining to my father all the reasons
why I probably would never make good
in the majors:
I was too small;
my fielding was atrocious;
nobody knew what I would look like
against really good pitching.
All in all, he insisted, it was a chancy thing.
But the Yankees were willing
to risk a *small* investment.

My father may have believed some of this
but I did not—
not about my being too small anyway.
Phil Rizzuto was holding down the shortstop post
with the Yankees at that time
and it would have taken one and a half of him
to match me in size.

And I was confident that I was as strong
as most big leaguers already.
Still I listened respectfully,
convinced that Mr. Greenwade really
believed what he was saying,
and conscious at least that my fielding
was a long way from major league quality.
My father agreed finally
that $1,100 would be an appropriate bonus
on such a doubtful prospect,
plus a $400 fee
for playing out the season in the minors,
and he had me put my name, along with his,
on the paper Tom Greenwade gave him.
It was not until the signing
was announced in the paper
and I read Tom Greenwade's prediction
that I would probably set records with the Yankees,
equaling Ruth's and DiMaggio's,
that I began to wonder
if my father and I had been outslicked.
Greenwade, by *his* account,
had just been going through Oklahoma
on his way to look over a *real* prospect,
when he stopped to talk to us.
I never did find out who that *real* prospect was.

But all this was no more than a passing irritation.
Just the chance with the Yankees
was all I wanted or felt I deserved.
I never for one moment
believed I would give Babe Ruth's records a run,
or even come close to matching Joe DiMaggio,
who was my own private hero.

Greenwade assigned me at once to the Class D club
in Independence, Missouri, of the K-O-M League,
and after I had had a few days' orientation
at the Yankee farm club in Joplin,
my father set out
to deliver my body to Independence.

This was the first time in my life
I had left home to stay
and I was not entirely easy in my mind about it.
I was glad my father
was going to drive me to Independence.
It was just seventy miles away.
But still, to be without my family, in a strange bed,
with ballplayers all probably much abler
and much older than I....

At Independence, we went together
to find the manager of the ball club, Harry Craft.
He greeted us in his hotel room,
with shaving cream all over his face.
Yet, despite his state of undress,
he had the same stern dignity about him
that my father had,
and a way of carrying himself that told you
here was a man of the kind you don't meet every day.
He shook my hand pleasantly
and let us sit down while he finished shaving.

"From now on," my father said,
"Mr. Craft is your boss.
I want you to do just as he tells you
and pay attention to what he says,
just as if I were saying it myself.

And I want you to play this game just the way
you would play it if I were here to watch you.
And to act in every way just as if I were right handy."
I promised that I would.
For I was struck nearly dumb now
with the solemnity of the occasion,
being an obedient son
and, at seventeen, young for my age,
as many a small-town boy was in that day.
Then my father shook hands and left me
and promptly I felt the beginnings
of that dreadful uneasiness that shy people suffer
when left suddenly in strange surroundings
with people they do not know.
I did not know where I was to sleep
or take my meals, or when,
and could not shame myself by asking.
For a long moment
I did not want to play professional baseball at all,
I just wanted to be home.
Mickey Mantle, 1967

74 In Special Olympics
    it is not the strongest body
    or the most dazzling mind that counts.
    There is the invincible spirit
    which overcomes all handicaps.
    For without this spirit
    winning medals is empty.
    But with it, there is no defeat.
    Eunice Kennedy Shriver, 1968

    Let me win
    but if I cannot win,
    let me be brave in the attempt.
    Special Olympics Oath

One of the many things
I have very much enjoyed about working
for the Space Agency and the Air Force
is that they have always given me free rein—
even to the extent of addressing
this most august assemblage without coaching,
without putting any words into my mouth.
Therefore, my brief remarks
are simply those of a free citizen,
living in a free country,
and expressing free thoughts which are purely my own.

Many years before there was a space program,
my father had a favorite quotation:
"He who would bring back the wealth of the Indies,
must take the wealth of the Indies with him."
This we have done.
We have taken to the moon
the wealth of this nation,
the vision of its political leaders,
the intelligence of its scientists,
the dedication of its engineers,
the careful craftsmanship of its workers,
and the enthusiastic support of its people.

We have brought back rocks,
and I think it's a fair trade.
For just as the Rosetta Stone
revealed the language of ancient Egypt,
so may these rocks unlock the mystery
of the origin of the moon,
and indeed even of our earth and solar system.

During the flight of Apollo 11,
in the constant sunlight
between the earth and the moon,
it was necessary for us to control the temperature
of our spacecraft by a slow rotation,
not unlike that of a chicken on a barbecue spit.
As we turned, the earth and the moon alternately
appeared in our windows.
We had our choice.
We could look toward the moon,
toward Mars,
toward our future in space,
toward the New Indies,
or we could look back toward the earth, our home,
with the problems spawned over more
than a millennium of human occupancy.

We looked both ways.
We saw both, and I think that is what our nation must do.
We can ignore neither the wealth of the Indies
nor the realities of the immediate needs
of our cities, our citizens, our civics.

We cannot launch our planetary probes
from a springboard of poverty,
discrimination, or unrest;
but neither can we wait until each
and every terrestrial problem has been solved.
Such logic two hundred years ago
would have prevented expansion westward
past the Appalachian Mountains,
for assuredly, the Eastern seaboard
was beset by problems of great urgency then,
as it is today.

Man has always gone
where he has been able to go.
It's that simple.
He will continue pushing back his frontier,
no matter how far it may carry him
from his homeland.

Someday in the not-too-distant future,
when I listen to an earthling step out
onto the surface of Mars
or some other planet,
as I heard Neil step out
onto the surface of the moon,
I hope I hear him say:
"I come from the United States of America."
Michael Collins, 1969

76   If you can dream it, you can do it.
Walt Disney

Dear Uncle Sam:
Since you have been the object
of much criticism lately,
both from within and without your borders,
I would like to write you a few words of praise
to brighten your New Year.

In the past two years I have travelled
in most all the countries of the world.
In most all the places I visited
I saw irrefutable evidence
of your deep concern for the welfare
of all the people of the globe.
Your men in uniform
are scattered throughout the world.
Not a one of them is there
to conquer any space
or subdue a human being.
They are at their assigned places
to insure that free men will remain free.
Many white crosses there
give evidence to the sacrifice made by those
who never returned to their homeland.
Twice in my lifetime
you have joined other free nations
to put down those
who would enslave their fellow man.
You beat your enemies to the ground
only to pick them up again
and dust them off,
bind up their wounds
and tenderly nurse them back to health again.

In many cases you provided them
with more modern and sophisticated equipment
than we have at home.
Your scientists, engineers and technicians
are busy all over the world today
to help people obtain a more abundant life.
Your doctors, nurses and many helpers
are fighting the effects of disease and poverty
in underdeveloped and, in some cases,
over-populated countries of the world.
Most of the people of the free world
appreciate this and praise you for it
and pray that you will not become
discouraged enough to cease your endeavor.
I pray for you and thank God for you, dear Uncle,
because you have done so much for me.

I was born in a tent in Oklahoma,
and grew up in poverty.
My parents were sharecroppers
and moved from farm to farm.
In the fall of 1922 they took their six children
and headed west and became migrant workers.
Seven or eight months later
we reached California in time
for the fruit harvest and became known,
along with others, as "fruit tramps."
The next year my parents separated
when I was ten years of age.
All the children,
ranging in age from two to fourteen,
went with my father
and for several years went back and forth
from Texas to California working our way along.

We went to school
when we were in one place long enough
for the truant officers to find us.
Getting an education under these conditions was difficult,
but with the help of many others
we all made it to high school...
Our father's health was not good
and he also developed a serious drinking problem.
The two youngest children had to be sent
to their grandparents for a while,
but we soon got back together again.
We finally settled down out west
and began our slow climb out of poverty.
Many people helped us along the way.
Thank you, dear Uncle,
for allowing God to bless us through you.

I sit today at the top of eight companies
one of which is doing business all over the world.
I do not claim even a small amount of genius for myself,
but would like to tell the world
that our system of government
gives a better chance
to the individual to have a good life
than any system known to man.
I do not belittle those
who have been unable to reach their goal
but offer my experience for their encouragement
and also to encourage those
who have it made to help those who don't.
I could never go back and find and thank all those
whose lives touched and enriched mine,
so to make up for it,
I will try to help and encourage others.

I count it a privilege
to support my church and other worthwhile causes.
I don't mind paying income taxes
because they are an indication of material blessings.
So, dear Uncle Sam,
don't let anyone tamper
with your system of government
unless they first show you a better one.
Thanks for listening and Happy New Year.

Sincerely yours,
Alton S. Newell, 1971

78 I have always felt
   that although someone may defeat me,
   and I strike out in a ball game,
   the pitcher on that particular day
   was the best player.
   But I know when I see him again,
   I'm going to be prepared.
   If he struck me out on a curve ball,
   I'm going to be ready for his curve ball.
   Failure is part of success.
   There is no such thing
   as a bed of roses all your life.
   But failure will never stand in the way of success
   if you learn from it.
   Hank Aaron

Two hundred years ago
we, the people
of the United States of America,
began a great adventure
which stirred the imagination
and quickened the hopes
of men and women throughout the world.
The date was July 4, 1776; the occasion,
the signing of our Declaration of Independence.
No other nation in history
has ever dedicated itself more specifically
nor devoted itself more completely
to the proposition
that all men are created equal,
that they are endowed by their Creator
with such unalienable rights
of life, liberty and the pursuit of happiness.

Two centuries later, as we celebrate
our Bicentennial year of independence,
the great American adventure continues.
The hallmark of that adventure
has always been an eagerness to explore the unknown,
whether it lay across an ocean or a continent,
across the vastness of space
or the frontiers of human knowledge.
Because we have always been ready
to try new and untested enterprises in government,
in commerce, in the arts and sciences
and in human relations,
we have made unprecedented progress
in all of these fields....

In the space of two centuries,
we have not been able to right every wrong,
to correct every injustice,
to reach every worthy goal.
But for two hundred years
we have tried
and we will continue to strive
to make the lives
of individual men and women in this country
and on this earth better lives—
more hopeful and happy,
more prosperous and peaceful,
more fulfilling and more free.
This is our common dedication
and it will be our common glory
as we enter the third century
of the American adventure.
Gerald Ford, 1976

I ran and ran and ran every day,
and I acquired this sense of determination,
this sense of spirit
that I would never, never give up,
no matter what else happened.
That day at Tuskegee
had a tremendous effect on me inside.
That's all I ever thought about.
Some days I just wanted to go out and die.
I just moped around and felt sorry for myself.
Other days I'd go out to the track
with fire in my eyes,
and imagine myself back at Tuskegee,
beating them all.

But looking back on it all,
I realized somewhere along the line
that to think that way wasn't necessarily right,
that it was kind of extreme....

I won all the rest of the races I was in
the rest of that season.
But I never forgot Tuskegee.
Wilma Rudolph, 1977

I am now fifty-nine years old,
which is an awkward age to define.
At fifty-nine, I am no longer middle-aged. I have, after all,
no 118-year-old elders among my acquaintances.
Yet I could hardly be called elderly.

An awkward age, then,
to define, but a delightful one to live.
I am aging from the neck up.
Which means I am elderly enough
to have attained a look of wisdom;
middle-aged enough to have a body
that allows me to do what I want;
and a face that lets me get away with it.

You know that look.
My hair is short and graying,
the face is just skin and bones,
the general impression of an ascetic
who began the fight with the Devil in the garden,
decided it wasn't worth it and walked away.
My latest picture, in fact,
looks a little like Teilhard de Chardin.
The look of a man with ideas so heretical
they bothered the Devil even more
than they did the Pope.
Preaching the perfectability of man
might not get you banished from Rome,
but it certainly would get you thrown out of hell.
And the look, too, of a man who forgave God,
and then his fellow men,
and finally himself, and then was free.

Well, you know I am not yet old enough
to look even remotely like that.
But fifty-nine leaves quite a bit of time to go.
Years that could be as exciting
as any that have gone before.

What will always remain an excitement is the race.
At fifty-nine, I am still the benchmark of performance
for any number of runners.
Over my fifteen years of running,
I have consistently year in and year out
been at the junction of the upper and middle thirds
of runners finishing in a race.
I have become the pass-fail mark
for my fellow runners.
If they beat me, they go home satisfied.
If I beat them, they hope to do better next time.
For my group, then, I am the top gun,
the man they call out for a showdown.

I am no easy mark.
I could give most readers of this book,
whatever their age, a five-minute head start
and run them down in twenty or thirty minutes.
I also have guts,
which is simply the decision to stand pain.

Some think guts
is sprinting at the end of a race.
But guts is what got you there to begin with.
Guts start in the back hills
with six miles still to go
and you're thinking of how you can get out
of this race without anyone noticing.

Guts begin when you still have forty minutes
of torture left and you're already hurting
more than you ever remembered.
Fortunately, guts seem to increase with age,
rather than decrease.
I may not want to wrestle with the Devil,
but I am willing to wrestle with myself.
And while I am beating myself,
I usually beat others as well.

Newcomers are usually easy to handle,
although I may have to pass them twice.
The first time anyone is passed by someone my age,
the natural reaction is disbelief
and a sudden sprint to regain the lead.
However, the next time I pass they usually give in,
resigned to the fact
that they are not yet ready to take the old man.

Some are injudicious enough to rile me up.
This summer, I was passed
at the halfway mark of a six-miler
by someone who said,
"I've been waiting to do this for three years."
I passed him back about a mile down the road
and now he'll wait another three years
before he gets near me again.

Of course, I have that same effect on others,
although I never say anything to upset anyone.
This year, for instance, at Westport in a ten-miler,
with about a mile to go,
I closed in on a running friend, a twenty-five-year-old,
whom I had never been near before in a race.

With about two hundred yards to go,
there were only fifteen yards
and three runners between the two of us.
As we entered the shopping plaza for the finish,
the other three runners passed him
and he did nothing.
He was, as far as I could see, dead in the water.
I cranked up,
and with a hundred yards to go I blew past him.
It was early, but it seemed safe.
Did I neglect to tell you I am also dumb?

I was about ten yards ahead
and apparently home free
when I heard this groaning, grunting animal
coming up on me.
He drew even
and as I glanced over I could see him,
wild-eyed, spittle all over his face,
and his face the picture of agony.
Then he was gone.

Later he told me
he had recognized the bald head
and there was no way I was going to beat him.

So it is not age that is threatened by youth,
but the other way around.
Youth is threatened by age.
From where I sit the fifties look great,
and I suspect the sixties will be even better.
I may not yet look like Teilhard,
but there's always this:
I will never again look like my high-school picture....

You are your only friend.
The only protector
of your body and its beauty.
The only defender
of your play and its delights.
The only guardian
of your childhood and its dreams.
The only dramatist and actor in your unique,
never-to-be-repeated living of your life.

Rise to that challenge.
Live your own life.
Success is not something
that can be measured
or worn on a watch
or hung on the wall.
It is not the esteem of colleagues,
or the admiration of the community,
or the appreciation of patients.
Success is the certain knowledge
that you have become yourself,
the person you were meant to be from all time.

That should be reward enough.
But best of all
is the fun while you are doing it.
And, at the very least, you will heal yourself.
George Sheehan, 1978

82   Let me start with the difference
between excellence and excellent.
Excellence is clearly something to strive for.
But *excellent* doesn't go far with me
because I am a product of the Chicago public schools
where we were graded with F, G, E and S—
fair, good, excellent and superior.
If you were only excellent you were not on the top.
James D. Watson

I've watched many people
in various lines of endeavor
striving to attain the best,
and I have tried to determine
what qualities they had in common.
Whether they were baseball pitchers
trying for a no-hit game,
runners attempting to break a world record,
or grape growers intent on producing
the finest wine in the world,
they all had complete dedication to their goals.
They displayed greater knowledge
than their competitors;
they were willing to put in the extra effort
necessary to approach perfection;
they never settled for second best.
They exerted themselves
to reach these heights of accomplishment
for both financial reward and esteem
of their peers or clients,
and for their own satisfaction.
Stanley Marcus, 1979

I really want my comic strip
to be the best comic strip there is.
Cartooning has a good deal of variety to it.
There is political cartooning,
gag cartooning,
illustrative cartooning
and all different kinds.
I am strictly a comic strip artist.
I just try to draw the best one there is.
That is all.
I have worked very hard to try to do this.
I try never to have any letdowns.
I try never to send in anything
that I am not totally satisfied with,
which is almost impossible,
and I rarely send in anything just to get by.
I'd rather fall a day behind in the schedule
than send in something
that I don't think is pretty good.
I think I'm competitive.
I regard the comic page
like a golf course or a tennis court.
I want to win on that comic page every day.
Charles Schulz, 1981

Let me say
that I have a real commitment to excellence;
but I think the motivation is,
clear and simple;
I think an individual ought
to make the most of his talents,
perfecting them
if they need perfecting,
enlarging them
if they are too parochial.
But he really is committed to making a contribution
and it can be in the widest variety of forms.
I am very, very catholic in my tastes,
and I like a good baker
who can bake a good loaf of bread,
or a man who runs a good fishing boat here,
or people who run a good restaurant.
I have never believed
that I was engaged in a profession
that was in any way sacrosanct or privileged.
I think I could have done just
as good a job as a banker,
or a newspaper editor,
or a college professor
or head of a labor union,
which I probably would have been
had I not been able to get a college scholarship.
I admired the labor union leaders of that era,
men like John L. Lewis and others.
I think they worked
in a very difficult "ambiente"
and a lot of them handled it very well, indeed.

And I think that could
have been a challenge to me.
In other words,
I really believe that one ought to capitalize
upon the talents that he has
and ought to try to make a contribution.
It's as simple as that.
James Michener, 1981

I believe that we need *leadership*
more than ever before.
Leadership.
Strong leadership.
We need to return the United States
to its position of power and influence in the world—
not for the purpose of warfare—
but for the purpose of having a strong defense
in order to *avoid* warfare,
and to regain the respect
that other nations had for us in the past.
We also need more pride in ourselves
as individuals within the country.
This should help not only individuals
but business and the economy and life in general.
We also need less government restrictions
so that business can improve
and enable individuals
to do their best in a free society.
There are too many umpires in the game today.
Joe DiMaggio, 1982

87 You give 100 percent
    in the first half of the game,
    and if that isn't enough,
    in the second half you give what's left.
    Yogi Berra

88 I think the American dream
    of always being number one in everything
    is not necessarily realistic.
    That should not be the goal.
    The ultimate goal should be
    doing your own best and enjoying it;
    participating in life and being honest and fair
    to everyone else as well as to yourself.
    That may sound strange,
    coming from such a competitor as I have been,
    but it is what I have learned and I really believe it.
    Peggy Fleming

The pleasure of risk is in the control needed
to ride it with assurance
so that what appears dangerous to the outsider
is, to the participant, simply a matter
of intelligence, skill, intuition, coordination –
in a word, experience.
Climbing, in particular,
is a paradoxically intellectual pastime,
but with this difference:
you have to think with your body.
Every move has to be worked out in terms
of effort, balance and consequences.
It is like playing chess with your body.
If I make a mistake,
the consequences are immediate, obvious,
embarrassing and possibly painful.

For a brief period,
I am directly responsible for my actions.
In that beautiful, silent world of the mountains,
it seems to me worth a little risk.
A. Alvarez, 1983

Don't listen to those who say,
"It's not done that way."
Maybe it's not, but maybe you will.
Don't listen to those who say,
"You're taking too big a chance."
Michelangelo would have painted the Sistine floor,
and it would surely be rubbed out by today.

Most important, don't listen
when the little voice of fear inside of you
rears its ugly head and says,
"They're all smarter than you out there.
They're more talented, they're taller,
blonder, prettier, luckier and have connections.
They have a cousin
who took out Meryl Streep's baby-sitter...."

I firmly believe
that if you follow a path that interests you,
not to the exclusion of love, sensitivity,
and cooperation with others,
but with the strength of conviction
that you can move others by your own efforts,
and do not make success or failure
the criteria by which you live,
the chances are you'll be a person
worthy of your own respect.
Neil Simon, 1984

I joined General George S. Patton, Jr.'s
Third Army headquarters
in Luxembourg early in 1945.
I never knew my commanding general,
never talked with him;
I gazed at him in wonder from afar.
His exploits were already legendary.

He was an imposing figure.
Whether riding in a jeep,
standing at attention,
or listening to a briefing, he dominated the scene.
His polished exterior glistened.
He was always on display,
his energy coiled like a cat's.
He bent his head to pray and also,
in the ample courtyard of the old people's home,
to let a French general,
who was decorating him, kiss his cheeks.
He inspired excitement and awe,
as well as loyalty and trust.

Duty there was like nowhere else.
The customary helmet
with rank painted on the front
was not good enough;
an ordnance shop welded on a gold bar for me.
The food was standard fare,
but the cooks were required to show imagination.
A slice of bologna
would be skewered by a toothpick
and served on a piece of toast.

In the mess hall,
the grand dining room of the Hotel Brasseur,
elderly civilian waiters wearing tails
served us in exquisite style.
We had special treatment, we were made to realize,
because we were special persons,
superior to the troops in the other armies,
and so we acted accordingly.
Despite our travels
through the mud of the springtime thaws,
we were neat and clean, on the qui vive.
I recall no griping.
I was, and still am,
proud to have been a member,
no matter how insignificant,
of the Patton team.
Like thousands of men
who still say with quiet satisfaction,
"I rolled with Patton,"
I have glad recollections.
His death was a personal loss,
and the news of it brought me close to tears....

George S. Patton, Jr.,
gained fame as a battlefield leader.
Ranking with the world's great army commanders,
he has been called
the greatest combat general of modern times
and the most inspiring.
Troop proficiency, discipline,
and determination were his trademarks.
No strategist or theorist,
Patton had few equals in preparing,
then directing men and units to fight in war.

His lifetime, from 1885 to 1945,
coincided with enormous transformations
in society, politics, and technology.
The United States moved into the industrial age
and emerged an international power,
and the U.S. Army
grew from a small and dispersed frontier force
into a huge mechanized establishment.
During this evolution, the transition
from the horse and the saber to the tank,
Patton played an important role.

In the course of his career, he mastered
the changing conditions and circumstances
of warfare in the twentieth century.
Serving in sequence as a cavalryman,
the foremost American tank expert,
and the leading exponent of armored action,
he participated in three armed conflicts:
the relatively primitive campaign in Mexico,
the massive confrontation on the Western Front,
and the challenging variety of operations
on the European side of World War II.
He occupied every grade
from second lieutenant to full general
and commanded units of every size
from platoon to field army.

He was thoroughly professional.
Even as a boy
he showed an interest in military matters
and a natural understanding of tactics and maneuver.
His school papers displayed his admiration
for Epaminondas' battle formations;

Julius Caesar's system of intelligence,
which gave him knowledge of enemy movements;
and, above all, Alexander the Great, who, Patton wrote,
"always aspired to perfection in everything."
The Athenians failed in their expedition to Sicily
(where Patton would later succeed)
because, according to Patton,
Nicias' procrastination "proved fatal."
Young Patton appreciated the value of the cavalry charge
as well as the use of concentrated forces.
Most important, he recognized what he called
"the undefinable difference
which makes a good or a great general."

Seeking to emulate the masters of the art of war,
Patton strove continually
to discover that "undefinable difference"
between the merely good and the sublime great
so that he himself could bridge the gap.
His constant reading in history and military affairs
presented him with a thorough understanding
of past warfare;
he alluded with authority
to the fighting skills of warriors
as various as Cossacks, Poles,
Turks, Arabs, Moors, and Moros.
He gave rapt attention to the martial skills
deemed necessary for each time and place.

But what set him apart from those
who were similarly schooled and obsessed
was his ability to transmit to his soldiers
a driving will to win.
It was the essence of his leadership.

This extra dimension
  derived from his unique character and personality.
  They were his own invention and creation
  and arose out of feelings of inadequacy.
  Shy and withdrawn by temperament,
  tending easily to tears of emotion,
  unsure of himself,
  sensitive to natural and artistic beauty,
  he scorned these characteristics.
"A man of diffident manner,"
  he once wrote, speaking of himself,
"will never inspire confidence.
  A cold reserve cannot beget enthusiasm" in combat.
  Thus, "the leader," he continued,
  referring to himself, "must be an actor,"
  have "the fixed determination
  to acquire the warrior soul,"
  and "is unconvincing unless he lives his part."

Seeing himself to be unfit
  because he lacked what he considered
  to be the military virtues,
  he struggled with single-minded devotion
  to remake himself, to alter his inner nature
  into his image of the fighting man.
  He consciously shaped the talents he had inherited,
  modified his strengths and outlook,
  stifled the qualities he regarded as unworthy,
  cultivated the traits he believed to be desirable,
  and periodically tested himself
  to see whether he measured up to his standards.
  No wonder he loved masquerade parties
  where he could dress as King Arthur or Ivanhoe
  and in an instant assume a new and faultless identity.

No wonder his behavior was unpredictable
and sometimes contradictory,
flamboyant on one occasion,
introspective on another.
Hot-tempered, sentimental, profane,
humble before God,
he was an exhibitionist who played to the gallery,
with his pistols and polished appearance his props.
Through the exterior of this exaggerated man,
who was larger than life to his children and colleagues,
peeped a barely controlled hysteria.
His extraordinary fluency with language,
his saucy wit,
his unexpected turns of phrase
covered his troubled interior,
where opposing inclinations battled for supremacy.
Toward the end of his life,
even he could barely distinguish his real self
from the portrait he had deliberately faked.

Sallie Flint, widow of Colonel Harry Flint,
a close friend of Patton's
who was killed while leading his regiment
in Normandy, said it best. She wrote,
"Few people outside of his family,
knew the gentleness, the true courtesy,
the almost puritanical uprightness and devotion
to his religious convictions
that were the real George Patton....
Underneath the seemingly rough and tough exterior
was the thoughtful, sympathetic,
almost boyish man....
The 'Blood and Guts' manner, the tough talking,
was really a sort of whistling in the dark

which he had from the very first
contrived to serve as a kind of apparatus
to build himself into the person he wanted to be
as a soldier...strong, physically, mentally, morally
(and he was all these)...
unmoved by fear and suffering,
the sight of death, blood, any horrible or vile thing....
This...was the motivation
back of all the rough, profane,
and at times vulgar manner and speech....
Underneath the rough-spoken, cold-blooded exterior
he was a gentle and kindly person
who had to make himself tough to do the job he had.
He wasn't born that way."

An extraordinary individual
both exuberant and meditative,
Patton carried with him a vision of his own fulfillment,
a Holy Grail he pursued with all his might.
He worked hard,
avoided relaxation,
feared complacency.
Every activity he chose to engage in
contributed to his mastery of warfare.
He had the good fortune to receive the opportunity
to perform on the field of battle
and, thereby, to achieve his ambition.
His victories in World War II turned him into a folk hero,
half man, half god,
a mythic figure who,
four decades after his death,
dazzles still the public imagination.
Martin Blumenson, 1985

If you think you are beaten, you are.
If you dare not, you don't.
If you like to win
but you think you can't,
it is almost certain that you won't.

If you think you'll lose, you're lost,
for out in the world we find,
success begins with a fellow's will—
it's all in the state of mind.

If you think you are out classed, you are.
You've got to think high to rise.
You've got to be sure of yourself
before you can ever win a prize.

Life's battles don't always go
to the stronger and faster man,
but sooner or later,
the man who wins
is the man who thinks he can.
Napoleon Hill

The person I am
is the sum-total of the life I've lived.
So, I have very deep emotions
about the blue Air Force uniform
that I wore most of my adult life.
The Air Force molded and trained me,
and who I am and whatever I've accomplished,
I owe to them.
They taught me everything
I needed to know to do my job.
There is no such thing as a natural-born pilot.
Whatever my aptitudes or talents,
becoming a proficient pilot was hard work,
really a lifetime's learning experience.
The best pilots fly more than the others;
that's why they're the best.
Experience is everything.
The eagerness to learn how and why
every piece of equipment works is everything.
And luck is everything, too.

Many pilots are killed
because they get into situations
where it is impossible to survive,
while others, because of luck
or knowing everything about their emergency gear,
slip between the raindrops.
I made my share of critical mistakes
that nearly cost me my life.
I climbed too steeply in the X-1A and paid for it
by being bashed around the cockpit
and scared out of my senses knowing I was going in.

To survive took everything I knew
and had ever experienced in a cockpit,
so that maybe one hour less flying time
could have been the difference
between drilling a hole or landing safely.
I saved myself by sheer instinct,
but a knowledgeable instinct,
based on hundreds of previous spin-tests.
Experienced at spinning down to earth,
I was less disoriented than others
who had done it many fewer times,
and was more likely
to make the right moves to save myself.

And luck.
The most precious commodity a pilot carries.
How can I explain
surviving the million-to-one odds against me
when my ejection seat
tangled in my parachute shroud lines
and set them smoldering,
to the point where after I landed
I pulled those burnt lines apart with a slight tug?
I can't explain it.
Nor can I explain
surviving intact after getting clobbered
by the rocket-end of that chair
and having my face set on fire.
To survive, fly again, and have no facial scars?
Luck, pure and simple.

The question I'm asked most often
and which always annoys me
is whether I think I've got "the right stuff."

The question annoys me because it implies
that a guy who has "the right stuff"
was born that way.
I was born with unusually good eyes and coordination.
I was mechanically oriented, understood machines easily.
My nature was to stay cool in tight spots.
Is that "the right stuff"?
All I know is I worked my tail off to learn how to fly,
and worked hard at it all the way.
And in the end, the one big reason
why I was better than average as a pilot
was because I flew more than anybody else.
If there is such a thing
as "the right stuff" in piloting,
then it is experience.
Chuck Yeager, 1985

I always taught players
that the main ingredient of stardom
is the rest of the team.
It's amazing how much can be accomplished
if no one cares who gets the credit.
That's why I was as concerned
with a player's character as I was with his ability.

While it may be possible
to reach the top of one's profession
on sheer ability,
it is impossible to stay there
without hard work and character.
One's character may be quite different
from one's reputation.

Your character is what you really are.
Your reputation is only what others think you are.
I made a determined effort to evaluate character.
I looked for young men
who would play the game hard, but clean,
and who would always be trying
to improve themselves to help the team.
Then, if their ability warranted it,
the championships would take care of themselves.
John Wooden, 1986

The world
is a reservoir of inspiration.
Our senses are constantly
inundated with images and sounds.
Everything is worthy of notice,
because everything can be interpreted.
Once, while I was trying
to explain this to some reporters,
a bird flew into the tree right above us
and began to sing the melody of a familiar tune,
in fact, one that *I'd* written years before
called "It's a Raggy Waltz."
Never had I been provided
with such an instant demonstration
of a point I was trying to make.
Had the bird learned the song from me?
Of course not.
Or had the song been planted in my subconscious
where it grew until the day I set it down on paper?

Discoveries in art as in science
require the willingness to take notice of everything.

Creativity is a process
that occasionally produces instant results.
But in my youth there was a time
when I would go for days afraid to write;
nothing I could think of seemed good enough.
I would stare at a blank piece of paper for hours,
searching for the right combination
of rhythmic, melodic, and harmonic ideas
swimming around in my head.

However I never became so frustrated
that I stopped trying.
Now after years of discipline,
the creative process rarely eludes me.
Writing down the ideas
and seeing a full score through to completion
can be an exhausting task.
The more hours my fingers
are locked in a writing grip,
the more necessary it is to compensate
with some five-finger exercises and scales.
Jazz is a special form of expression
because so much of it is improvised.
I must constantly prepare
for the moments of immediacy
between fingers and mind
when proficiency allows musical creativity
to emerge freely.
Dave Brubeck, 1986

If you're to be a successful leader
you must have integrity.
People must know
what to expect from you.
Once you make a commitment
to a person or a task,
you must honor it.
I try to live by that,
down to the smallest detail.
I return phone calls promptly;
I answer letters;
I meet deadlines.
I work at doing things right the first time,
and everybody knows it.
To me, there's no greater compliment
than for people to say,
"I can always count on Buck Rodgers."
It's a matter of living up to your word,
time after time.
And since the people I work with
can count on me,
I feel I have every right
to expect as much from them.
Buck Rodgers, 1986

97 Winning is living.
Every time you win, you are reborn.
Every time you lose, you die a little.
George Allen, 1986

98 I want world class people
in this institution.
I don't care where you find them
or what they're doing,
but if they've got brains and they meet the test
we'll find a job for them to do.
People are the most important asset
of any company.
And I want the best!
Walter Wriston, 1986

Whoever said,
"It's not whether you win or lose that counts,"
   probably lost.
   There are winners, and there are losers.
   And if you chose
   to be one of the former,
   the journey through life
   can be a little lonely.

When you're a winner,
   you have to set the standard for excellence
   wherever you go.
   You have to battle against the fatigue,
   the intimidation,
   the human tendency
   to just want to take things a little easier.
   You have to be able to come up with,
   time and again,
   one consistently great performance after another.
   It's grueling.
   And I don't know many people
   willing to make the effort.
   But it's those few true professionals
   you meet along the way
   that help make the journey
   just a little easier to manage.
   Martina Navratilova, 1987

Anyone who knows
the meaning of excellence
speaks my language.
I made a discovery recently
about the word excellence.
While it loosely translates
into all 2,796 languages spoken today,
few people seem to grasp its meaning.

Now you don't need to be a linguist
to appreciate the problem.
If you've ever ordered a cab *pronto*
and had to wait,
or expected dinner *extraordinaire*
and wound up with potluck,
you know what I mean.

No doubt,
the confusion surrounding excellence
upsets linguists and laymen alike,
but I think what sustains us
are those few professionals
who are able to convey
the real meaning of excellence
without ever having to say a word.
Charles Berlitz, 1987

Excellence: An American Treasury

Afterword

Anyone who works in the vineyard of ideas as a means of livelihood for very long will usually begin to acquire more than a little respect for, if not a bit of insight into, how the creative mind works.

The fact is, no one really knows for sure how or why it works, except that, at its very best, it can produce results that are marvelous if not miraculous.

If there is a failsafe system for creative thinking, surely it must be a combination of a scavenger hunt, a wild goose chase, a multiple choice test, and maybe even a game of musical chairs.

The nicest thing about the creative mind is that if you treat it right, it will give you honest answers. It will tell you when you are on the right track and when you are not. When you are not is the easiest of the two. It is simply a brick wall at the end of a blind alley. You will know when it stands as an obstacle in your path.

Knowing when you have found the pot of gold at the end of the rainbow, however, takes a little more perception. Sometimes it takes the vision to see an exit sign in the first light of day along a highway of no return, but it is always a detour well worth taking. For there is always a magnificent sunrise. You simply will not be able to miss it.

The creative task involved in producing the book at hand presents an interesting example, the starting point being a fundamental question: How do you illustrate a contemporary book on the subject of excellence?

We thought about the question for what seemed to us to be longer than usually required for a similar creative challenge. Were we losing our capacity to visualize the alternatives? The best thing to do, we concluded, was simply to get moving. As usual, we began to go down one road and another, and we were not surprised to notice the presence of a familiar sign: *dead end*.

But we were not discouraged. The human mind is more wonderful than the world's most advanced computer, and a computer will never replace it for the human mind lets you scan your own life's experience. In our case, it took us back to an earlier day when we were working on a different kind of creative challenge.

It was World War II. We were twelve years of age. We were there at the kitchen table. We had just opened a packet of postage stamps. We were placing the stamps very carefully with tweezers and gummed hinges into the pages of a new stamp collector's album. We were quite pleased. We had saved our pennies and had sent in the order form for a complete set of stamps called *The Famous Americans* series. And today, they had arrived, the great American authors, inventors, poets, musicians, artists and statesmen. It was a moment to remember.

Suddenly, it is 1988 again. Could it be that *The Famous Americans* stamp series is what we were searching for?

We ordered a current stamp catalog from the Postal Service. We wanted to see what had happened to the series after the war. The catalog arrived. We found that it had been continued. How would we select precisely which individuals most exemplify excellence? How would we integrate the portraits from the stamps with the verbal commentaries on excellence?

Was there a way to accomplish with one visual element what we already knew could be accomplished using many? It was then that a strong, vibrant visual image, quite unlike any of the others, seemed to command our attention from the pages of colorful stamp reproductions in the catalog, and the image was familiar, as if meeting by chance a good friend from the past, and in one way it was. It was Bradbury Thompson's famous postage stamp, *Learning never ends*. Why had we not thought of it before? It seemed exactly right for the frontispiece of our new book. We called Bradbury at his home in Riverside, Connecticut. We asked him for some background on *Learning never ends*, and we knew he would have it. Brad is the most prolific of American stamp designers, officially credited with more than ninety stamps. He readily complied, and an interesting story began to unfold.

As background, in addition to being a talented stamp artist, Bradbury Thompson is one of the most important graphic designers of the twentieth century. He has been Westvaco's design consultant for more than fifty years. He has been responsible for numerous innovative design projects for the company, one of the most notable being the development along with Jean Bradnick of the initial concept of the Westvaco Americana series of limited editions for which he served as the designer for the first twenty-six volumes. Thompson has, in addition, a distinguished career as art director of leading American magazines and sacred works, most notably, the Washburn

College Bible, in which the words are typeset in the cadence of speech, a unique approach in publishing the Bible.

Josef Albers, Thompson's friend, fellow member of the faculty of the Yale School of Art and a collaborator on the Washburn College Bible, died in 1976, not long after he had signed the frontispieces for the Bible. Several of Albers' admirers proposed to the U.S. Postal Service that a stamp be issued to honor this influential teacher and artist, considered by art historians to be the father of optical art. However, there is a statute that prohibits the issue of a commemorative stamp until at least ten years after the individual's death. Thompson did not forget his friend. In 1980, when the Postal Service commissioned a stamp to honor the newly established Department of Education, he took advantage of this opportunity to remember a great teacher. Thompson adapted a vivid Albers painting entitled *Homage to the Square: Glow* from the series of Albers' studies about the independence and interdependence of colors. The painting shows a red square surrounded by three more squares that progress through shades of orange from dark to light. The Secretary of Education was happy to interpret it as a symbol of the new department itself, "starting from a deep solid base and reaching out to more and more people each year, spreading a glow throughout American education." That seemed a long leap in interpretation for some, but it was indeed a handsome stamp and a loyal tribute to a fellow teacher and artist.

As a happy coincidence, 1988 represents the centennial of Josef Albers' birth as well as the centennial of our company's founding. (Somebody must be looking out for us.) It also marks the publishing date of *Bradbury Thompson: The Art of Graphic Design* by Yale University Press, a significant contribution to the history of graphic design, an undertaking which Westvaco has supported wholeheartedly. This elegant book, itself a landmark in the history of fine bookmaking, brings together for the first time a full spectrum of Thompson's timeless contributions to American graphic design, including his important work for Westvaco. A chapter entitled, *A Love of Books,* expresses the philosophy of the Westvaco limited edition series, the design of classic literature in classic format.

We were very fortunate over the years to have worked alongside this master designer, observing his working methods and philosophy of design in actual practice. One of Thompson's hallmarks has ever been a classic adaptation of typography to the modern world. In 1978, in *Emerson Essays,* for example, in order to enhance readability and comprehension and to energize the power of each thought, Thompson set the lines of type in unequal length, each containing a complete phrase, as if the words might have been spoken. A decade later, in 1988, we find it appropriate to again use this timeless approach in the typographic treatment of this volume. The Sabon type, of noble classic origin was originally cut in about 1532 by Claude Garamond, and was updated by Jan Tschichold in recent years. Its use in the flush left, ragged right format enlivens the language, makes the text more logical and enhances the poetic flow of each passage. As the designer develops a sensitive ear to the spoken word, the full drama and excitement of our language can be enhanced greatly by the careful display of the printed word on paper. It takes long, meticulous effort to do this effectively which is undoubtedly the reason few designers follow this course. But, it is such a logical thing to do, and the final result always seems to make a real difference.

There is much more that we could say about the philosophy and detail of design execution that went into the preparation of the volume, but if we said more, we might run the risk of either boring you or maybe even giving away a few trade secrets that help build into our books the kind of competitive edge that we like to incorporate into all of our Westvaco products.

Suffice to say, we look forward eagerly to working on next year's Christmas book. It will be a creative challenge. *Learning never ends*.

Excellence: An American Treasury

Acknowledgments

Every effort has been made to trace the ownership
of all copyrighted selections appearing in this book.
Grateful acknowledgment is made to the following
companies, publishers and individuals for their
permission to reprint this material:

Atheneum Publishers,
an imprint of Macmillan Publishing Company
for *Confessions of an Advertising Man*
by David Ogilvy, © 1963 David Ogilvy Trustee

Atlantic-Little Brown
and Rosemary A. Thurber
for *My Years With Ross*
by James Thurber, © 1959,
renewed 1987 Rosemary A. Thurber

Bantam Books, a division of Bantam,
Doubleday, Dell Publishing Group, Inc.
for *Yeager: An Autobiography*
by General Chuck Yeager and Leo Janos, © 1975

Dave Brubeck

Burson-Marsteller
for *Why Leaders Win Price Wars*
by William A. Marsteller, © 1960
and *How to Grow a Great Salesman*
by John C. Callihan, © 1966

Center for Dewey Studies
Southern Illinois University at Carbondale
for *Democracy and Educational Administration*
from *Later Works of John Dewey*
by John Dewey, © 1937